# Ice Cream and Other Frozen Delights

# Ice Cream and Other Frozen Delights

**photography by Mike Cooper**

*For Veena,*
*and in memory of Albert, who first led the way.*

First published in Great Britain
in 2013 by Absolute Press, an imprint of
Bloomsbury Publishing Plc

**Absolute Press**
Scarborough House
29 James Street West
Bath BA1 2BT
Phone  44 (0) 1225 316013
Fax  44 (0) 1225 445836
E-mail  info@absolutepress.co.uk
Website  www.absolutepress.co.uk

**Publisher**
Jon Croft
**Commissioning Editor**
Meg Avent
**Art Director**
Matt Inwood
**Project Editor**
Alice Gibbs
**Editor**
Eleanor van Zandt
**Photographer**
Mike Cooper
**Food Stylist**
Genevieve Taylor
**Indexer**
Ruth Ellis

The rights of Ben Vear to be identified as the
author of this work have been asserted by
him in accordance with the Copyright
Designs and Patents Act 1988.

A catalogue record of this book is available
from the British Library

**ISBN: 9781906650858**

Printed in China by C&C Offset Printing Co. Ltd

**A note about the text**
This book was set using Century. The first
Century typeface was cut in 1894. In 1975 an
updated family of Century typefaces was
designed by Tony Stan for ITC.

**Bloomsbury Publishing Plc**
50 Bedford Square, London WC1B 3DP
www.bloomsbury.com

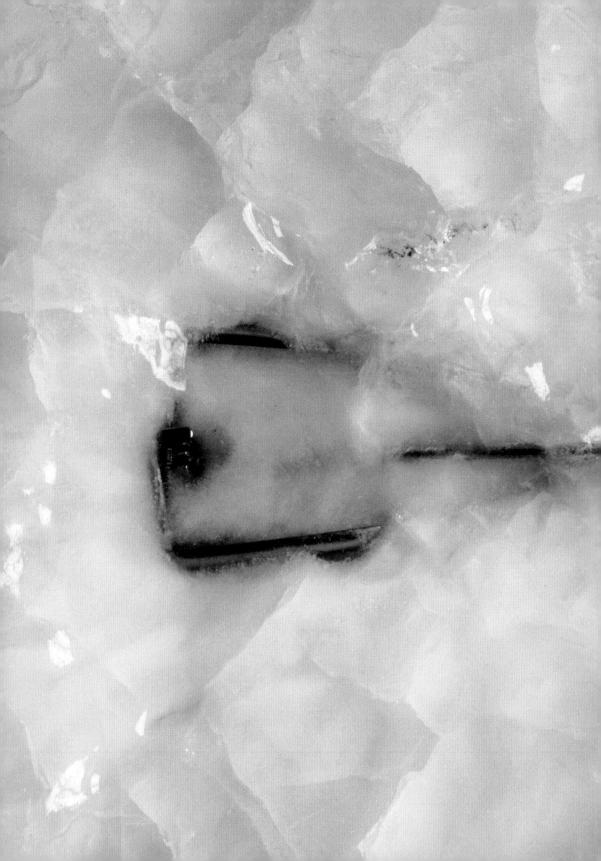

introduction

# *Like most people, I fell in love with ice cream as a child...*

I well remember joyfully running out into the road on Sunday afternoons to meet the ice cream man. However, in my case the ice cream man was a member of my family – sometimes my uncle, or my dad or, usually, my granddad.

My clan, the Winstones, have been making ice cream in the Cotswolds since 1925. Our factory, near Stroud, supplies luxury ice cream to food retailers throughout the land, and many people flock to our own little shop to buy it directly from us. It's always gratifying to see how excited people can get as they tuck into a scoop or two of our Rum & Raisin, for example, or Butterscotch Chip.

Gratifying, but not really surprising. At its best, ice cream offers a delicious, multi-sensory experience, appealing to more than just our taste buds. Its smooth, melting texture also tantalises our sense of touch; its delicate fragrance, derived from any of innumerable different flavours, charms our sense of smell; and its beautiful colours and glistening surface entice our eyes.

When, in the past, ice cream was still a rare luxury, difficult to produce and enjoyed only by the rich, it was held in high regard. An aura of mystery hung around this seemingly magical confection. At the very least it was considered one of life's great sensual pleasures. The eighteenth-century French wit Voltaire once observed, 'Ice cream is exquisite; what a pity it isn't illegal' – implying that this would make it even more seductive.

Well, all that has changed. Today supermarket cold cabinets are filled mainly with imitation ice cream produced using a cocktail of different chemical emulsifiers, preservatives, artificial flavourings and enhancers. Much of this air-filled pap has never come close to a cow. Clearly, when it comes to ice cream (and many other foods as well) we have lost our way.

Fortunately, quality ice cream is now making a comeback. Various new artisan ice cream producers have started up in recent years, and my own company is flourishing and growing. But, depending on where you live, if you want to buy really good ice cream in a wide range of flavours, you may need to seek it out – and, admittedly, spend a bit more money.

That's where this book comes in. The following pages contain one hundred of my recipes for ice creams, sorbets and other frozen treats which you can easily make, at relatively little expense, in your own kitchen. All you need is some good ingredients, basic kitchen equipment (an ice cream maker, though useful, is not essential) and a little patience. Once you've understood and practised the basic techniques (explained on pages 24–30), you can use these to create your own variations and original, unique flavours.

I hope this book will help you to discover – or rediscover – the pure pleasure of eating truly delicious ice cream.

# *For thousands of years people have enjoyed eating something cold and sweet...*

The ancient Romans are known to have stored ice from the mountains in vast ice houses and sweetened it with honey and fruit, making something similar to what we know today as a granita. The Persians had their own form of water ice, made with snow. However, the first appearance of something resembling ice cream seems to have been in China, during the Tang dynasty (618–907), when emperors and their courtiers ate concoctions made of milk from cows, goats and even buffaloes, frozen and sweetened with sugar, herbs and spices. Somewhere along the way, again probably in China, it was discovered that adding salt to ice caused it to melt more quickly, at the same time causing the creamy mixture contained inside it, when repeatedly stirred, to freeze into a smooth, semi-solid consistency.

According to legend, it was the Venetian explorer Marco Polo who, in the thirteenth century, brought the secret of making ice cream from the Far East back to Europe. Whether or not this is true, it does seem to have been the Italians who launched 'iced cream' in the West, as well as water ices, flavoured with fruit and, often, spirits. Labour-intensive and costly, ice cream was for many years enjoyed only by the top people. It reached the French court sometime in the seventeenth century and soon spread to other royal tables. One observer, reporting on a banquet for King Charles II at Windsor Castle in 1671, remarked that guests at the King's own table (only) were presented with 'One Plate of Ice Cream'.

By the early eighteenth century, the secret of making ice cream was beginning to circulate more widely. A French pamphlet entitled *L'Art de faire des Glaces* ('The Art of Making Ice Cream') appeared around 1700. Published in England in 1718, *Mrs Mary Eale's Receipts* included some recipes for ice cream. Such publications were eagerly snapped up by affluent gourmets who wished to impress their friends.

Increasingly the 'must-have' amenity on one's country estate was an ice house. Typically a cave dug into the earth, this was filled with ice gathered from ponds and lakes during the winter and used throughout the year for cooling bottles of wine and making ice cream.

Quickly removed to the kitchen, the ice was placed in a large bucket or other container around a smaller cylindrical container, called in French a *sorbetière*, which was then filled with the cooked and cooled ice cream mixture and constantly turned by hand. Frequent stirring of the contents with a spatula or other utensil introduced air into the mix and ensured that it was frozen evenly (essentially the same principle used by modern electric ice cream machines). When partially frozen, the ice cream would usually be packed into a fancy mould, replaced in the ice until set, unmoulded and finally presented to one's suitably awed dinner guests.

The Americans were not slow to discover the pleasure of ice cream. Several of the Founding Fathers had ice houses, among them Thomas Jefferson, at his Virginia estate, Monticello. After a diplomatic visit to France in the 1780s, during which he learned to make ice cream, Jefferson brought home a sorbetière and a French recipe for vanilla ice cream. This was for the traditional style of ice cream, using egg yolks, sugar and cream to make a custard base.

Meanwhile, farther north, in Philadelphia, a lighter form of ice cream, made without eggs or sometimes only with egg whites, was becoming popular. It is still known today as Philadelphia-style ice cream, while the custard-based ice cream, as in Jefferson's recipe (and nearly all of those in this book), is often called French-style.

From the beginning of the nineteenth century, ice cream parlours began to spring up in the United States, as well as in Europe, so that this delicacy could be enjoyed, as a special treat, by the general public. By the end of that century, with the advent of mechanical refrigeration, it had become possible to produce ice cream economically on a large commercial scale. Even so, the hand-cranked churn (a refinement of the sorbetière) remained in use for domestic and small-scale production well into the twentieth century.

The democratisation of ice cream continued with street vendors. Many of these, in Europe and North America, were Italians, who hawked their product by crying, '*O che poco!*' ('Oh, how little!', referring to the price), which got corrupted to 'hokey pokey', a disparaging term for the cheap ice cream they sold. Ice cream was also often sold in a small, thick glass called a 'penny lick'; after consuming the meagre contents, the customer returned the glass, which was then used, often inadequately washed, for the next customer. This unhygienic practice was eventually replaced by the use of paper cups and edible cones. Beginning in 1920, the Good Humor man, selling chocolate-covered vanilla ice cream on a stick and similar treats, became a familiar sight on American streets, while in Britain a host of different ice cream manufacturers, large and small (including one Albert Winstone) brought ice cream to the public. The heyday of the British ice cream van lasted well into the 1970s; at one point there were as many as 50,000 of them traversing Britain – a stark contrast to the mere 5,000 or so today.

The most popular mobile ice cream in Britain was – and remains – the Mr Whippy. Like its American counterpart, Dairy Queen, and other soft-scoop ice creams, this consists of a base mix of cream, sugar, milk, flavouring and a stabilising agent (in place of eggs), pumped through a compressor-based machine which at point of dispensation injects air into the ice cream mix to expand the product and give it a soft, light texture. The process behind the Mr Whippy was initially developed in the 1950s by a team of research chemists at J Lyons and Co, including a young Oxford graduate called Margaret Thatcher, as part of an effort to increase the level of calcium in children's diets.

The inter-war years in the United States saw a proliferation of soda fountains – partly, during the 1920s, as an alternative to the disappearance of bars (apart from speakeasies) during Prohibition. Americans fell seriously in love with ice cream in all its guises, from the multitude of flavours available (one restaurant chain offered 28 flavours), to elaborate concoctions like sundaes and ice cream sodas – a love affair that continues today.

In Britain, towards the end of the twentieth century, ice cream manufacturers were seeking more ways of cutting the cost of production with greater automation and reductions in ingredient quality – including the use of whey powders, chemical stabilisers and flavour enhancers. More recently a return to quality is evident, not only in ice cream but in food generally. Artisan ice cream makers, committed to using locally sourced, organic ingredients and innovative techniques, are producing luxurious ice creams and sorbets in a dazzling range of flavours – restoring a little of the excitement that marked the first appearance of ice cream hundreds of years ago.

# *It all began with my great grandfather Albert Winstone, back in the 1920s...*

For many years he had worked as a french-polisher for a local piano works near his home in the Cotswolds, in Gloucestershire. Then, following a fire, the company closed down, and Albert, along with the rest of the workforce, found himself unemployed.

After struggling to find other work, Albert finally decided to capitalise on his own premises: an old Victorian coach house perched on the edge of the rolling green expanse known as Rodborough Common, overlooking Stroud's Five Valleys (an area familiar to readers of Laurie Lee's novel *Cider with Rosie*). Many walkers, ramblers, golfers and other locals passed near his house on their way to this common land, and Albert reasoned that they would be glad of some refreshments on the way. So he and his wife, Doris, set about selling cups of tea, cakes and a variety of sweets, some home-made, to this passing trade.

Although this enterprise was popular with the locals, Albert felt that something a bit more exciting was needed. So, using an old Victorian recipe handed down through his family, he mixed up a batch of vanilla ice cream. It was a great success, and soon the cakes and sweets were forgotten about and Albert's focus shifted firmly to ice cream. This was in 1925. Next to his home he built a small shop, where he sold 'Winstone's Ice Cream' to an ever-increasing clientele.

With the help of Doris, his brother-in law Lewis Cook and a few friends, he produced all of the ice cream on his kitchen stove, refining the original recipe to his own satisfaction and churning it on a hand-cranked churn.

The next step, of course, was to market his ice cream to a wider public. With the profits from the shop he bought himself a motorcycle and a sidecar and then used his DIY skills to convert the sidecar into a makeshift freezer unit, complete with a dry ice compartment. He would slot in his ice cream churn and ride up and down the Stroud valleys, pulling up alongside schools, houses and individual customers, amid the clouds of smoke backfiring from the motorcycle, to dispense his ice cream. He would scoop the ice cream into whatever receptacles people brought out to him: glass or ceramic bowls, plastic containers or metal dishes. Often, if he hadn't already been flagged down, Albert would ring an old iron hand bell to signal his arrival.

And so the years passed, with business ticking over comfortably. In 1952, the hand bell was replaced by a less-appealing mechanical chime, part of Albert's first, refrigerated, ice cream van. With this major investment, the company's business began to grow rapidly, and more family members got involved. Albert's son Frank (my grandfather), my father, Colin Vear, and my Uncle John came on board. By the 1970s Winstone's had a fleet of vans and were upping production and tentatively starting to sell wholesale to restaurants, supermarkets and garden centres. Still operating from its base at Rodborough Common, the company bought out rivals in Cheltenham and Gloucester. Along with increased volume came recognition of the quality of our ice creams. Beginning in the 1960s, Winstone's regularly won awards in national competitions, as we still do today.

By the 1990s Frank had inherited the business to become managing director. The van operation had reached a high point, with 25 of our white, green and red vehicles travelling the roads of Gloucester and Wiltshire over 50 different routes. But the heyday of the vans was soon to end. Hefty charges and bureaucratic restrictions began to be imposed by local authorities, while fuel costs soared. Ice cream, of sorts, was ever more widely available from the burgeoning supermarkets, making the mobile trade increasingly redundant. By the end of the decade Winstone's had said farewell to more than half of its vans.

Now the company became almost entirely a wholesale business, and so we have remained, while still serving customers who turn up at our Cotswold shop. My mother, Jane Vear (Albert's granddaughter), now manages the company, alongside my brother Tom, who looks after sales and operations, and my father, Colin, who acts as the company's general manager, while I deal with branding and retail. I also roll up my sleeves and work on developing new flavours, many

of which feature in this book. For these small, experimental batches I use the sort of equipment found in most domestic kitchens, as well as one of Albert's original Gusti batch freezers, which dates from the late 1950s and sits in our factory. I feel that there's something very special about using the same machine that Albert used all those years ago.

New flavours are very important to our business, of course. Vanilla may still be the most popular flavour nationwide, but such innovative concoctions as our Rhubarb Crumble, Blackberries & Cream and Honey & Ginger, now give it stiff competition, while seasonal flavours, such as Mixed Spice Winter Ice Cream, enjoy a moment of popularity in their turn.

To make sure that the quality matches the variety, we seek out the best possible ingredients, focusing on local sources. Where possible we forage for the fruits and herbs we use in our kitchen, as well as shopping at the fantastic Stroud Farmers' Market and in a number of the delis and farm shops dotted around the county. And, of course, we use only the finest Cotswold water and local organic milk and double cream from a beautiful herd of Longhorn cows who graze on grassland just a couple of kilometres from Winstone's factory.

Although still a small company, with about 20 staff, Winstone's produce more than 1,000,000 litres of ice cream a year, consumed by an estimated 200,000 people. Business can be hectic at times, especially when, on occasion, something goes wrong: a batch is over- or under-flavoured or a delivery vehicle breaks down, followed by a mad rush to ensure our stockists get their orders on time. Weekends are normally a bit more relaxed, as some of us don aprons to serve customers in our shop.

Despite the long hours, it's a hugely satisfying job. How many people are lucky enough to earn their living by giving other people a bit of instant happiness? That's how we Winstones and Vears and all the rest of the team feel about ice cream. And so, after more than 85 years of doing this, we thought it was time to share our expertise and our love of good ice cream with a wider public – you, the readers of this book.

**Above:** Three of the four generations of family who have kept Winstone's a family-run business: (from left) my dad, Colin Vear; me; my mum, Jane Vear; and my grandad, Frank Winstone.

# *On the face of it, ice cream might seem to charm us by artistry...*

A few of our ancestors believed that charm to be magic. The real truth is that there is an awful lot of science which goes into the processes of both making and enjoying it.

## *The science of taste*

When a spoonful of ice cream – or any other food – enters our mouth, it triggers many different taste receptors. The most noticeable of these form part of the fungiform papillae: tiny mushroom-shaped protuberances located on the top front section of the tongue. These papillae sometimes swell a little when stimulated by a strong flavour – for instance, a strong sour citrus flavour. Other papillae and taste receptors are found elsewhere on the tongue and in other parts of the mouth and throat. Different types of taste buds are receptive to different kinds of taste.

It has long been thought that all tastes could be categorised into four primary tastes – salt, sweet, sour and bitter – and combinations of these. Although these four tastes do indeed represent distinct perceptions, in fact people experience a variety of additional tastes, such as astringency (cranberries and tea), pungency (hot peppers and ginger), fat, starch, and metallic tastes. Also, mixtures of various chemicals may elicit entirely new taste sensations, making it impossible to estimate the actual number of distinct tastes, which may run into the thousands.

However, it is not our taste buds alone which provide us with a sense of taste; these work in tandem with our sense of smell, through the olfactory system in our nose, which detects scent, and our eyesight, which stimulates the gustatory cortex, located at the centre of our brain, helping process taste. Information on the texture and temperature of food and other factors is also processed in the gustatory cortex.

We're familiar with the role that smell plays in the experience of taste, but our eyesight plays a surprisingly important part in this process, working with the gustatory cortex to stimulate our taste buds and trigger memories of previous tastes and textures which we have previously enjoyed – or not enjoyed. Ice cream manufacturers are able to exploit this by producing ice creams and sorbets in colours that will stimulate a positive reaction and encourage us to buy or sample them.

## The science of ice cream

My interest in science goes back to my boyhood, when it was my favourite subject at school. Today, I apply it to my work developing new ice cream flavours and textures and altering the state of a variety of ingredients to achieve different results.

I got my first taste of the science behind food when I bought a very early edition of Mrs A. B. Marshall's *The Book of Ices*, first published in 1885, which gives five hints on making ice cream, Victorian style:

*(i) Too much sugar will prevent the ice from freezing properly.*

*(ii) Too little sugar will cause the ice to freeze hard and rocky.*

*(iii) If ices are moulded, freeze them in the freezer to the consistency of a thick batter before putting them in moulds.*

*(iv) If they are to be served unmoulded, freeze them drier and firmer.*

*(v) Broken ice alone is not sufficient to freeze or mould the ices: rough ice and salt must be used to set ices solid.*

With some modifications, these rules still apply today; simply mixing together the core ingredients and freezing them does not make a good-quality, scoopable ice cream. For good results we must balance ingredients to create the perfect micro-structure of air, liquid, fat globules and small ice crystals which will hold together in a balanced matrix.

Essentially ice cream is composed of three constituent states of matter: solid (typically ice crystals, fat globules and undissolved sugar), liquid (typically milk, water and sugar solution) and air, which is added to the ice cream mixture by the process of churning. To make good ice cream, we need to know how these ingredients behave. For example, the fat content of ice cream, derived from milk, cream and eggs, and found in some other ingredients, such as chocolate, will give density and a smooth texture and help the ice cream stay cold. Achieving the correct fat content, of around 7–10 percent, is important; if the content is too high it may produce an unpleasant texture of crystallised fat globules.

Solids are also found in sugar, which is able to absorb several times its volume in liquid. Importantly milk, whipping cream and both double and single cream are also sources of solids. These solids are also known as milk solids, non-fat, or MSNF. A good source of MSNF is skimmed milk powder, which is easily available in most supermarkets and online. This contains no fat globules and so is an easy way to achieve perfect ice cream with a low fat content.

The interaction of these ingredients takes place during the mixing and especially the cooking. Here it is vital to apply patience: overheating the mixture will cause the base mix to burn; heating it too quickly will make it curdle.

When the ice cream mixture is placed in an ice cream maker, two complementary physical processes take place. The fluid surrounding the inner container (in earlier times the salted ice) begins to melt, by drawing heat from the surrounding materials, including the inner container (this is called an endothermic, or heat-absorbing change). The ice cream mixture loses heat through the wall of its container (called an exothermic change) and eventually reaches its freezing point.

At the same time, the paddles of the ice cream maker are stirring the mixture, which ensures that all of it has contact with the walls of the container and freezes evenly. The stirring also breaks up large ice crystals into small ones and introduces air into the mixture, giving it the characteristic smooth texture. Further freezing will make it more solid.

But when the ice cream enters our mouth it quickly absorbs some of our body heat and melts – delightfully.

# To make wonderful ice cream, you first need to understand the basics...

There are several different basic methods of making ice cream. In this book, nearly all of the recipes are of the French custard style, using egg yolks, sugar and cream. A few of them use gelatine or pectin, instead of eggs, to thicken the mixture (see, for example, Twenty-first Century Whippy, page 278); some use both gelatine and egg yolks (such as Birthday Cake Ice Cream, page 59); one uses a soft cheese (Dulce de Leche and Mascarpone Ice Cream, page 99).

Once you've acquired an understanding of the way levels of fat, solids and liquids can be adjusted to create different tastes and textures, you can create your own flavours. To start with, though, it's best to try some of the recipes in this book, which will give you practical experience of how these various ingredients and mixtures behave.

## The four basic steps of making ice cream

The process of making the ice cream will vary, depending on the ingredients used and the style of the ice cream. Here are the basic steps for making a custard-style ice cream; the last three steps are much the same for any kind of ice cream or sorbet.

### 1. Cooking

This usually involves gently cooking milk and cream together in a saucepan, sometimes with the addition of one or more flavourings, such as vanilla; then combining egg yolks with sugar to make a thick, glossy paste; incorporating the (reheated) milk mixture, slowly and carefully, with the egg mixture; and, finally, returning the combined mixture to the pan and cooking it until it reaches a custard-like consistency. To test for this stage, one lifts the mixing spoon out of the mixture and runs a finger over the back of it; if the finger leaves a clear mark, the mixture is ready.

### 2. Cooling

The cooked mixture is then poured into a container of some kind, such as a large jug or bowl, and left to cool to room temperature; then it is covered and placed in the refrigerator for at least an hour to chill. The chilling is an essential step to prepare it for the freezing process.

### 3. Churning

The mixture is poured into an ice cream maker (see page 32) and left to churn and partially freeze. It is this step – which usually takes 30–40 minutes – that gives the ice cream its smooth, light texture.

### 4. Freezing

In most cases the ice cream should then be decanted into a suitable container or an ice cream mould, covered with a lid and placed in the freezer to set solid. This will take at least 1 hour.

Finally, once removed from the freezer, the ice cream will need to be left for about 15 minutes at room temperature to soften, so that it can be scooped out easily. In my opinion, it deserves to be presented beautifully – perhaps with a topping of some kind, such as a fruit coulis, and/or some textural contrast, such as biscuits or meringues.

### Making ice cream without a machine

This process is relatively labour-intensive, but with patience and a bit of muscle power you can make quite acceptable ice cream this way.

First prepare the mixture and cool it, as for steps 1 and 2 above. Then place it in a large freezer-friendly container, cover it and place it in the back of the freezer for 1 hour.

Remove the container from the freezer and whisk the mixture vigorously with a fork to aerate it and break up the ice crystals. At this point the recipe may direct you to add inclusions, such as nuts or chocolate chips.

Return the ice cream to the freezer for another hour, then remove it and whisk again. Repeat this last step once more, then leave the ice cream in the freezer to set solid. In some cases it may be desirable to whisk it 4 or even 5 times; 3 times is the minimum.

## *Making a custard-style ice cream*

1. Break eggs into a bowl  2. Separate the yolks  3. Combine with caster sugar  4. Whisk yolks and sugar into a smooth paste  5. Pour milk and double cream into a saucepan and gently simmer  6. Scrape the seeds from a vanilla pod into the milk-cream mixture and continue to simmer and stir

**7.** Back to the yolk and sugar paste... **8.** ...fold it into the milk-cream mix **9.** Whisk in the pan to ensure the mixture combines well **10.** Once thickened, remove from heat and pour into a bowl **11.** Once cooled, cover with cling film and store in the fridge for 1 hour **12.** Decant mixture into an ice cream maker and freeze following the manufacturer's instructions

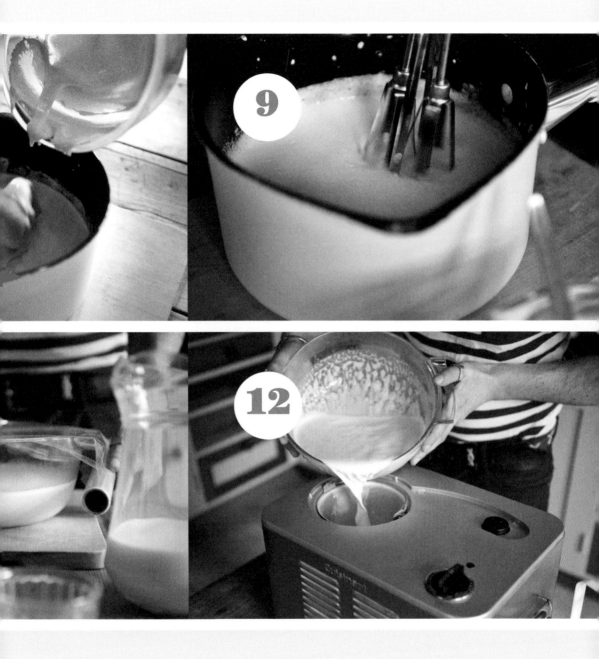

## Special techniques

Successful ice cream requires patience and the use of a few simple techniques. Here are three things you should know before starting out.

### Flavour maturation

Flavouring additions, such as vanilla, and solid inclusions, such as fruit, need time to infuse, or release their flavours into the base mix. Some of this will be achieved during the cooking, but the process continues during the cooling stage. After making an ice cream base, I allow plenty of time for the flavour to mature before churning – normally overnight; but a little extra time chilling in the refrigerator will certainly help to develop the flavour.

### Whisking

A key step in making the base mix for a custard-style ice cream is whisking the egg yolks and sugar to form a pale, thick, glossy paste. You can use a hand, or balloon, whisk for this or an electric mixer, whichever you prefer. Experience will tell you when the egg mixture is ready for the milk mixture to be added.

### Saving a curdled mixture

Occasionally mistakes will happen, and one of the hazards in making a custard base is allowing the egg mixture to curdle or form solid clumps, resembling scrambled eggs. If this starts to happen, quickly plunge the bottom of the pan into a sink partly filled with cold water, then blitz the contents in a blender or food processor. Finally, strain the custard back into the pan through a fine sieve and resume cooking – carefully this time!

If the mix is seriously curdled, you'll probably have to throw it out and start from scratch.

# You'll need a few pieces of kit, too...

Relatively few pieces of kitchen equipment are needed for making ice cream. As I've already noted (page 25), you don't actually need an ice cream maker, although you'll produce a smoother, more consistent ice cream if you do use one of these. So let's start by looking at the kinds of machines available today.

## Ice cream makers

Basically, most domestic ice cream makers fall into two categories.

The simpler kind consists of a drum-shaped bowl which must be placed in your freezer for eight or more hours before you plan to use it. This freezes the liquid in the cavity between the bowl's inner and outer shells. The motor and paddles are then attached to the bowl, the ice cream mix is poured in and the freezing and churning of the ice cream takes place. A variant of this bowl form of ice cream maker fits on to a stand mixer. After about half an hour, usually, the ice cream is thick and semi-solid, ready to be placed in the freezer. The advantage of this kind of ice cream maker is that it takes up little space on the kitchen counter and can be put away in a cupboard when not in use; it's also relatively inexpensive. The drawback is that you must remember to freeze the bowl well ahead of making the ice cream and make room for it in your freezer.

The more expensive type of ice cream maker has a built-in compressor which will freeze the base mix as the machine churns away. Most of these have an automatic timer or cycle, so that you can put your feet up and relax without keeping track of the time. Here again, usually once the cycle is complete the mix will need to sit in the freezer for a couple of hours. As a general rule, these automatic models produce a smoother-textured ice cream than do the simpler bowl-type ice cream makers. Some automatics include two containers, enabling you to make two batches of ice cream at once. Their drawback, apart from the price, is that they take up rather a lot of counter space.

However, if you are likely to make regular batches of ice cream for home or commercial use, and are even thinking about ice cream making as a potential future career, I advise you to invest in a high-end machine with a long warranty and the ability to make sizeable batches.

## Other equipment

Of course you'll need basic kitchen equipment, including a good-quality, heavy-bottomed saucepan, one or more large mixing bowls, a chopping board, wooden spoons, scales and measuring spoons and jugs. The following items will also be useful on occasion.

### bain marie
the double saucepan kind, also called a double boiler, e.g. tempering chocolate; a mixing bowl placed over a large saucepan can substitute

### blender/food processor
a necessity for creating many different flavours, especially those with fruit or nut inclusions; a powerful one, at least 750W, will be able to break down even the toughest fruit

### electric mixer and/or hand whisk
for beating egg yolks and sugar in making the custard mix; also for whipping egg whites and cream; which you choose for a given task is usually a matter of personal preference

### freezer-friendly container such as a plastic bowl with a lid
essential for freezing churned ice cream or sorbet

### ice cube tray
for freezing sorbet to use in drinks

### jug, large
cooked ice cream mix can be poured into this for cooling and chilling, then easily poured into the ice cream maker's container

### loaf tin
for freezing parfaits; should contain at least 1 litre and have a non-stick coating for ease of use

### melon baller
for scooping out small portions of ice cream for decorative effects, or for amuse-bouche servings

### moulds
various kinds, for making ice lollies, kulfi and, if you like, fancy shapes

### piping bag
for soft-serve ice cream and applying whipped cream decoration

### plastic (or wooden) spoon
for removing ice cream from ice cream maker without damaging its lining

### shot glasses
for amuse-bouche servings of ice cream or sorbet

*sieve*
for straining out solid items no longer
required, such as vanilla pods

*sugar thermometer*
essential for tempering chocolate and making
sugar syrup for e.g. caramel

*sundae, banana split dishes*
for elaborate ice cream desserts

*syringe*
for inserting filling into an ice cream shape

*toffee hammer*
for breaking up slabs of toffee; alternatively
a rolling pin can be used, over a tea towel

*waffle iron for cones*
special round-shaped type with shallow
indentations specifically made for this
purpose (there are many good online
suppliers selling the Cloer one which I use at
home); should have a non-stick surface

*And finally – a scoop!*
Aesthetics are important, and the visual
element plays a big part in the enjoyment of
ice cream. If you want your ice creams and
sorbets to look as good as mine do in these
pages, buy a high-quality scoop such as my
Zeroll (www.zeroll.com).

# *Every great ice cream begins with great ingredients...*

The following list includes most of the ingredients used for the recipes in this book. You may discover others in the course of creating your own ice creams, sorbets and other sweet concoctions.

I choose my ingredients based on seasonality, quality, flavour and, of course, previous results, using, wherever possible, organic and fair-trade products. I also make a point of buying ingredients from local producers, and I urge you to do the same wherever feasible. Producers who support your own local community and operate on a fair and ethical basis are worth supporting as much as possible.

### *Air*
Although not a product one can purchase, air is essential to achieving a perfectly smooth texture in ice cream or sorbet. The inclusion of air is achieved by an ice cream machine or through whisking by hand. In some cases, extra whisking by hand, after machine churning and before the mixture has set solid – called over-churn – is recommended in order to create an even smoother texture (see Birthday Cake Ice Cream, page 59).

### *Alcohol*
The addition of spirits and other alcohols can give an extra dimension to ice creams and sorbets, as some of the recipes in this book demonstrate. Where I live, in the West Country, we are fortunate in having good-quality ciders, perries, craft beers and wines close to hand. Where spirits have been used, I have attempted to source the best possible artisan brands, such as William Chase's innovative potato-based vodka, 'Chase Vodka'. It's worth splashing out extra money to up the quality of your ice cream or sorbet mix.

### *Berries and other fruits*
Many different kinds of berry can be successfully used in ice creams and sorbets. Apart from their flavours they provide interesting textures and, in many cases, wonderful colour.

Between the months of June and November I forage in the local hedgerows for gooseberries, red currants, blackberries, raspberries and wild cherries, as well as other fruits such as apples and plums. Of course markets and supermarkets can supply a profusion of fruits. As always, you should look for top quality, preferably organic and in season.

### *Botanical infusions*
Quite apart from the vast range of fruits, herbs and spices, the plant kingdom can offer many less familiar ingredients to tempt the ice cream maker. In the chapter devoted to these ingredients (see pages 213–229) you'll find intriguing recipes using all sorts of products from tea leaves to olive oil.

### Chocolate

In addition to choosing chocolate that is organic and fair-trade, you should make sure that it contains no less than 60 per cent cocoa solids; 70–75 per cent is usually recommended. Cocoa beans from different parts of the world will offer a wide range of flavours to suit different palates – from sweet, smoky, earthy chocolates through to bitter, spicier flavours. A full discussion of this ingredient can be found on pages 110–111.

### Citrus

Oranges, lemons, limes and other citrus fruits have long featured in sorbets, less often in ice creams. But several of the recipes in this chapter (see pages 165–187) use them in ice cream, where they impart a fresh, tangy quality to the creamy base.

### Cocoa powder

In her book *Momofuku Milk Bar* (2012) Christina Tosi recommends always to use unsweetened, alkalised cocoa powder, which has a neutral PH content, unlike processed cocoa powder, commonplace on supermarket shelves. This will help you achieve better, smoother, more consistent results in your ice cream making and baking efforts. I always use Valrhona cocoa powder, which is dark, rich and perfectly balanced.

### Dairy products

Milk and cream are, of course, essential ingredients of ice cream; double cream is especially useful for its rich, thick texture. In making ice cream, both at home and at Winstones, I source these from a local dairy whose products are pasteurised, but not homogenised and are produced by the farm's small herd of 50 home-bred traditional dairy Shorthorn cows.

For hundreds of years Shorthorn cows were the backbone of dairy farming in rural England; the Shorthorn breed is perfect for a truly organic farming regime.

### Condensed milk

As the name implies, this is milk that has been thickened through evaporation; it is also sweetened. It has a variety of uses and is sometimes used in making ice cream.

### Non-dairy alternatives

Instead of using dairy-based milk or cream, you can choose from an array of really very good non-dairy alternatives, which are readily available and affordable. These include cashew milk, rice milk, soy milk and coconut milk. Coconut oil also acts as a good substitute for double cream and is available online in powder or paste form.

### Eggs

Most of the recipes in these pages call for the use of eggs – usually just the yolks. In my kitchen I use eggs from Cotswold Legbar hens. Legbars (which include several breeds) were introduced to the United Kingdom from Patagonia in the 1940s; the Cotswold breed lay beautiful eggs which have an unusual soft blue shell and superb flavour.

### Flour

Recipes for biscuits, waffle cones and some other Accompaniments (see pages 259–275) will of course require flour. I source this from nearby Shipton Mill, a family mill who produce award-winning organic flour and can trace their roots back as far as the compiling of the Domesday Book in the eleventh century.

### Gelatine/Pectin

These are both thickening agents – the first animal-derived, the second plant-derived, which are widely used to make jellies as well as ice cream. They are both available in powdered and sheet (or leaf) form. I prefer the latter, as I find it easy to store and less messy than the powder, but in most cases you can use either.

#### Using powdered gelatine/pectin

This should be dealt with in two stages. First sprinkle the gelatine/pectin on to about 2 tablespoons of cold water and leave to soak for a few minutes. Then add this solution to the ice cream base, or other liquid, and stir over heat until it is fully dissolved and the liquid begins to thicken and become almost elastic.

#### Using sheet gelatine/pectin

To use, simply place the sheet of gelatine or pectin in the liquid (typically milk and cream) you are using for your ice cream base before heating it. Then gently warm the liquid and stir the leaf until fully dissolved.

### Herbs and spices

Virtually unlimited flavours can be achieved with the subtle use and mingling of these aromatic ingredients. We all know that mint goes with chocolate, but how about chocolate and rosemary (page 113)? Ginger is, of course, a perennial favourite in ice cream; a lime sorbet flavoured with chilli and fresh basil (page 204) is something else again. Make sure that your spices have not passed their 'use by' date.

### Sugar

For the recipes in this book I've used several different kinds of sugar. White caster sugar is required for nearly all of the recipes; it is finer and more easily dissolved than ordinary granulated (used occasionally, especially for some of the Accompaniments, pages 259–275). Muscovado sugar and light brown sugar, including demerara sugar, are used where a deeper flavour is desired, as in some of the spice-flavoured ice creams.

*Caramel*

This ingredient is produced by boiling sugar – often brown sugar – and can be used to make toffee and other rich-flavoured inclusions for ice cream. A full discussion of this ingredient can be found on page 82.

*Vanilla sugar*

Often used in place of, or in addition to, a vanilla pod or vanilla extract, vanilla sugar is a good way to add greater depth of flavour and some subtle sweetness to your ice cream. It's really very simple to make and a good way to re-use left-over vanilla pods. Take a 2kg Kilner jar or similar and place three or four vanilla pods (either new and unsplit, so they can be opened later for a recipe, or previously split and used) upright in the jar; fill the jar to the top with caster sugar, leave for at least a fortnight to allow flavour maturation and use whenever needed.

*Lavender sugar*

Like vanilla sugar (if less versatile), this will add extra depth and complexity to your ice creams, producing a sweet and aromatic taste. First, if using lavender from the garden, ensure that it is fully dried out. Stand four or five sprigs upright in a Kilner jar or similar and fill to the top with caster sugar. Leave for at least a fortnight to allow flavour

maturation, then use whenever needed. After use, remember to top the jar back up, ready for next time.

*Alternatives to sugar*

As part of a programme to develop a range of healthier ice creams, I've discovered a couple of good alternatives to sugar. One of these is xylitol, a natural product found in the fibre of birch, which is safe for diabetics and also good for your teeth. Similarly stevia, a herb, and agave, a succulent plant, are both good alternatives to sugar, containing fewer calories.

*Vanilla*

Available in its natural form as a pod or as the extract derived from the pod, this is an essential ingredient, not only for vanilla ice cream but for many other flavours as well. A full discussion of this important ingredient can be found on pages 44–45. One caution: avoid vanilla 'essence', which is a synthetic product.

*Every ice cream recipe in this book makes 1 litre of ice cream*

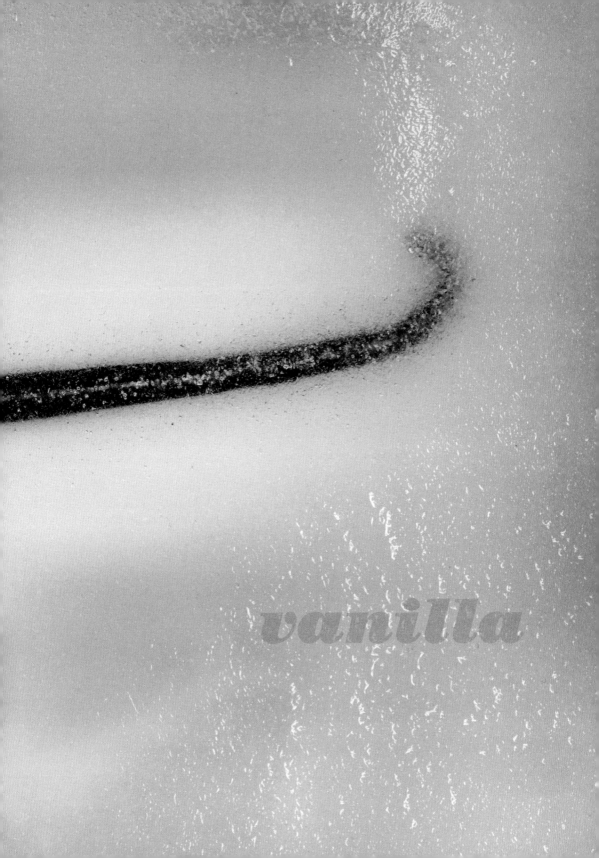

vanilla

The cultivation of vanilla, a kind of orchid, is extraordinarily labour intensive and in almost all cases requires growers to meticulously hand pollinate each vanilla orchid flower. Distinctively flavoursome, vanilla is perhaps best described in *The Flavour Thesaurus*, by Niki Segnit as 'rich, earthy and spicy'. The deeply perfumed, often smoky flavour of vanilla lends itself well to sweet dishes, which perhaps explains why it still remains the world's most popular ice cream flavour.

## A turbulent history of vanilla

The use of vanilla may originally have been discovered by the Totonac Indians of Mexico. Later it was acquired by the Aztecs, when they conquered the Totonacs in the fifteenth century, and still later was brought back to Spain by Hernán Cortés in the sixteenth, after his years of conquest in the New World. Before conquering the Aztec civilisation, Cortés and his men supposedly witnessed the Aztec emperor, Montezuma, drinking a beverage made from cocoa and water, flavoured with dried vanilla beans. Cortés brought the plant and pods back to Spain, along with cocoa. There it became an expensive luxury enjoyed only by the rich and the nobility, due in part to its high price and rarity.

For many years the Spanish were able to hold a monopoly on vanilla production, thanks to their control of Central America and Mexico.

This was because this region was the natural habitat of the melipona bee, the main pollinator of the vanilla orchid. It wasn't until the nineteenth century that a way was found to hand-pollinate vanilla in significant quantities and produce it in other parts of the world.

## Vanilla goes global

This breakthrough was achieved, amazingly, by a 12-year-old boy. Edmond Albius was a slave on the French island of Bourbon – now Réunion – in the Indian Ocean. Some vanilla orchid plants had been brought to the island in the early nineteenth century, but getting the short-lived flowers to bear fruit proved difficult. Introduced to plant cultivation by his master, a horticulturist, Edmond devised a technique of using a thin bamboo skewer to lift the membrane separating the vanilla flower's anther, which bears the pollen, from the stigma, where it can germinate, and then using a fingertip to transfer the pollen. His method is still used to hand-pollinate vanilla today.

After Albius's remarkable discovery, the island of Réunion briefly became the world's largest supplier of vanilla before being overtaken by the East African island nation of Madagascar. Today Madagascar still accounts for half of the global production of vanilla; other producers are Uganda, Mexico, India and Indonesia.

## Choosing the right vanilla

When making ice cream I use Madagascan 'Bourbon' vanilla; its sweet, complex taste lends itself well to ice cream, producing several subtle flavour notes which add depth to ice cream. Madagascan vanilla pods also work extremely well when used with brown sugar, adding sweetness to the caramel flavours produced in the cooking process.

Most of the flavour of a vanilla pod is contained in the seeds. So to use the pod you must first slit it open lengthways, using a sharp, short knife. Press open the two halves, then scrape out the seeds using the blunt edge of the blade. Submerge both pod and seeds in the ice cream mix, then, when directed by the recipe, lift out the pod. You can use the leftover pods to make vanilla sugar (see page 39).

The creation of a full-bodied ice cream, called 'flavour maturation' (see page 30) is especially important in the case of vanilla. Leaving the vanilla pod within the ice cream base for up to 24 hours, as I often do, will ensure that the full flavour of the vanilla is infused within the base mix, bringing out the subtleties of the smoky, earthy and spicy flavours. However, the seeds that remain in it will contribute greatly to the end result.

Flavour maturation can be achieved much more quickly by using vanilla in liquid form. I use a pure vanilla extract, which is produced by macerating and distilling vanilla at a very high temperature. My preferred brand is Ndali vanilla extract, which comes from a historic plantation in Western Uganda amid the explosion craters of a volcanic field. Ndali is one of only a handful of Fairtrade vanilla extracts available in UK supermarkets.

Be careful not to confuse vanilla extract with vanilla essence. This is a synthetic solution of vanillin in some form of alcohol, usually ethanol, and is inferior to vanilla extract in taste and quality.

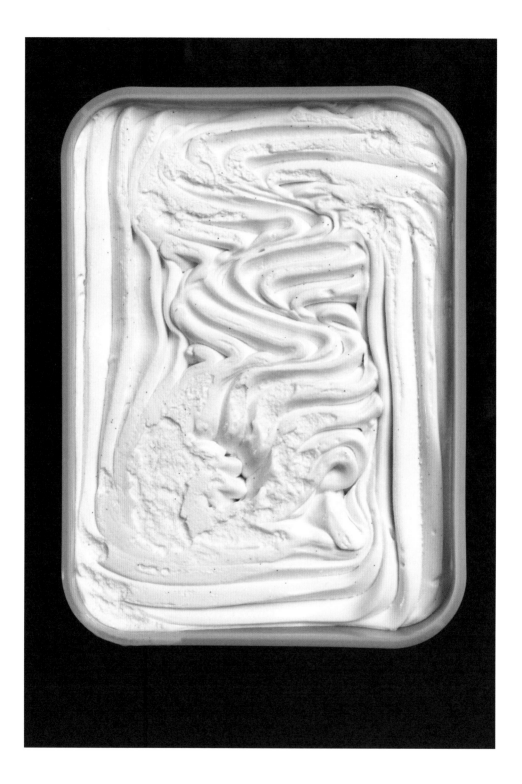

# basic vanilla ice cream

The pure, simple and instantly recognisable flavour of vanilla ice cream holds a precious place in most people's memories. Fuss-free and easy to make, this basic, traditional vanilla ice cream has no fancy inclusions and is based on my great-grandfather's original, award-winning recipe, which dates back to the 19th century.

250ml double cream
200ml whole milk
120g vanilla sugar (see page 39)
1 teaspoon fresh lemon juice
1 teaspoon vanilla extract
5 free-range egg yolks
2 tablespoons skimmed milk powder

Pour the cream and milk into a medium saucepan; add half of the vanilla sugar, the lemon juice and the vanilla extract, and place over a low-to-medium heat. Stirring at regular intervals, bring the mixture to a simmer; leave it at a simmer (but do not allow to boil) for 5 minutes, then remove from the heat and set aside, remembering to stir occasionally.

Place the egg yolks and sugar in a mixing bowl and whisk together, using a hand or electric mixer, until you have a pale, thick and glossy paste.

Bring the milk mixture back up to a simmer, then gradually pour it into the egg mixture, whisking all the time, until it is well incorporated.

Return the mixture to the saucepan and cook for about 10 minutes on a low-to-medium heat, stirring constantly, to prevent it from curdling, until it has thickened enough to coat the back of the spoon. Remove from heat.

Pour the mixture into a bowl or large jug and leave it to cool at room temperature. Then cover it with cling film and place it in the refrigerator to chill for at least 1 hour.

Following the manufacturer's instructions, pour the chilled mixture into your ice cream maker and set it to churn. Once it has finished churning, decant the partially frozen ice cream into a freezer-friendly container and leave it in the freezer to set solid.

If you do not have an ice cream maker, follow the instructions on page 25.

Remove the ice cream from the freezer about 15 minutes before serving so that it can soften slightly.

# bourbon vanilla ice cream

Using Madagascan, or 'Bourbon', vanilla, this luxurious, creamy and extremely simple vanilla ice cream is an indulgent and up-to-date take on my great-grandfather's recipe. Smooth, sweet and totally delicious, it's made using large quantities of eggs, cream and milk for a thick and creamy texture.

500ml double cream
400ml whole milk
1 vanilla pod
180g caster sugar
6 large free-range egg yolks
1 tablespoon Madagascan vanilla extract

Pour the cream and milk into a medium or large heavy-based saucepan. Using a sharp knife, split the vanilla pod in half lengthways, then use the blunt edge of the knife to scrape out the seeds. Add the pod and the seeds to the pan and tip in half the sugar.

Place the pan over a low-to-medium heat and bring to a simmer, stirring frequently to ensure that the mixture doesn't burn; do not allow it to boil. Let it simmer for about 5 minutes, then remove from the heat and set aside, remembering to stir occasionally.

Place the egg yolks and sugar in a mixing bowl and whisk together, using a hand or electric mixer, until you have a pale, thick and glossy paste.

Bring the milk mixture back up to a simmer, then gradually pour it into the egg mixture, whisking all the time, until it is well incorporated.

Return the mixture to the saucepan, add the vanilla extract and cook for about 10 minutes on a low-to-medium heat, stirring constantly, to prevent it from curdling, until it has thickened enough to coat the back of the spoon. Remove from heat and scoop out the vanilla pod.

Pour the mixture into a bowl or large jug and leave it to cool at room temperature. Then cover it with cling film and place it in the refrigerator to chill for at least 1 hour.

Following the manufacturer's instructions, pour the chilled mixture into your ice cream maker and set it to churn. Once it has finished churning, decant the partially frozen ice cream into a freezer-friendly container and leave it in the freezer to set solid.

If you do not have an ice cream maker, follow the instructions on page 25.

Remove the ice cream from the freezer about 15 minutes before serving so that it can soften slightly.

# *skinny vanilla ice cream*

Ice cream is special, a real indulgence and a treat, but for those of you watching the waistline, this low-calorie take on traditional vanilla ice cream will be welcome. Here, caster sugar is replaced with fruit sugar, whole milk with skimmed milk and cream delicious virgin coconut oil. All of these ingredients are widely available in health-food shops and some supermarkets, and all are totally natural.

20g virgin coconut oil
300ml skimmed milk
5 tablespoons skimmed milk powder
120g fruit sugar
1 tablespoon vanilla extract
4 free-range egg yolks

Pour the coconut oil, skimmed milk and skimmed milk powder into a saucepan and place over a low heat, stirring ocassionally until the coconut oil has melted into the milk. Once well combined, pour in half of the fruit sugar and the vanilla extract, stir to combine and bring the mixture to a simmer. Simmer, but not boil, for 10 minutes, then remove from the heat.

Place the egg yolks and remaining sugar in a mixing bowl and whisk together until you have a pale, thick and glossy paste.

Bring the milk mixture back up to a simmer, then gradually pour it into the egg mixture, whisking all the time, until it is well incorporated.

Return the mixture to the saucepan and cook for about 10 minutes on a low-to-medium heat, stirring constantly, until it has thickened enough to coat the back of the spoon. Remove from heat.

Pour the mixture into a bowl or large jug and leave it to cool at room temperature. Then cover it with cling film and place it in the refrigerator to chill for at least 1 hour.

Pour the chilled mixture into your ice cream maker and set it to churn. Once it has finished churning, decant the partially frozen ice cream into a freezer-friendly container and leave it in the freezer to set solid.

If you do not have an ice cream maker, follow the instructions on page 25.

Remove the ice cream from the freezer about 15 minutes before serving so that it can soften slightly.

# cornish-style dairy ice cream

This ice cream is a rich, indulgent affair, made with lashings of double cream, eggs and clotted cream (the Cornish element), with just a hint of vanilla. Over-churning is key to creating a thick, smooth consistency. This recipe is another adaptation of a Victorian classic used by my great-grandfather Albert in the 1920s.

300ml double cream
400ml whole milk
1 teaspoon vanilla extract
120g golden caster sugar
2 large spoonfuls of thick clotted cream
4 large free-range egg yolks

Pour the double cream, milk and vanilla into a medium or large heavy-based saucepan; tip in half the sugar and the clotted cream. Place over a low-to-medium heat and bring to a simmer, stirring frequently to ensure that the mixture doesn't burn; do not allow it to boil. Let it simmer for about 5 minutes, then remove from the heat and set aside, remembering to stir occasionally.

Place the egg yolks and sugar in a mixing bowl and whisk together, using a hand or electric mixer, until you have a pale, thick and glossy paste.

Bring the milk mixture back up to a simmer, then gradually pour it into the egg mixture, whisking all the time, until it is well incorporated.

Return the mixture to the saucepan and cook for about 10 minutes on a low-to-medium heat, stirring constantly, to prevent it from curdling, until it has thickened enough to coat the back of the spoon. Remove from heat.

Pour the mixture into a bowl or large jug and leave it to cool at room temperature. Then cover it with cling film and place it in the refrigerator to chill for at least 1 hour.

Following the manufacturer's instructions, pour the chilled mixture into your ice cream maker and set it to churn. Once it has finished churning, decant the partially frozen ice cream into a freezer-friendly container and leave it in the freezer to set solid.

If you do not have an ice cream maker, follow the instructions on page 25.

Remove the ice cream from the freezer about 15 minutes before serving so that it can soften slightly.

# *curiously healthy coconut ice cream*

Many ice creams are claimed to be 'healthy' and are proudly displayed as such in the health-food freezer section of supermarkets and health food shops. In most cases, though, these are simply lower in calories than most ice cream. Using now widely available ingredients, such as virgin coconut oil and xylitol (a sugar substitute relatively safe for diabetics and beneficial for teeth), I've made an ice cream that actually is good for you, and also rather delicious.

300ml cashew milk
20g skimmed milk powder
120g xylitol
20g virgin coconut oil
1 tablespoon vanilla extract
1 teaspoon guar gum
2 tablespoons unsweetened desiccated
   coconut

Pour the cashew milk, skimmed milk powder and xylitol into a saucepan and place over a low heat, stirring until all of the xylitol and skimmed milk powder is fully dissolved. Remove from the heat and set aside to cool.

Now add the coconut oil, vanilla extract and guar gum to the mixture, return to the heat and bring to a gentle simmer, stirring occasionally until all of the ingredients are fully combined and the mixture is thick enough to coat the back of a spoon for a few seconds.

Pour the mixture into a bowl or large jug and leave it to cool at room temperature. Then cover it with cling film and place it in the refrigerator to chill for at least 1 hour.

Pour the chilled mixture into your ice cream maker and set it to churn. While the mixture churns, sprinkle in the desiccated coconut; the paddle will ensure that the coconut is mixed evenly throughout the ice cream. Once it has finished churning, decant the partially frozen ice cream into a freezer-friendly container and leave it in the freezer to set solid.

If you do not have an ice cream maker, follow the instructions on page 25.

Remove the ice cream from the freezer about 15 minutes before serving so that it can soften slightly.

# vanilla and tonka bean ice cream

Smoky, earthy and sweet, the tonka bean is often used in perfume and cookery and is enormously popular in France. Native to South America, it is a short, black, shrivelled bean similar in both appearance and taste to vanilla. In this ice cream it works with the vanilla to create a spicy flavour full of sweet treacle-like undertones.

600ml double cream
200ml whole milk
1 teaspoon vanilla extract
1 tonka bean, grated
5 free-range egg yolks
125g caster sugar

In a saucepan heat the cream, milk, vanilla and grated tonka bean together over a medium heat for up to five minutes, stirring constantly to ensure that the cream does not boil or separate.

Place the egg yolks and sugar in a mixing bowl and whisk them together, using a hand or electric whisk until you have a thick, pale and smooth paste.

Pour the hot milk mixture slowly onto the egg mixture, whisking constantly to prevent curdling. Once the ingredients are fully combined, pour the mixture back into the pan and cook gently over a low heat, stirring constantly. When the mixture is thick enough to coat the back of a spoon, remove from the heat.

Pour the mixture into a bowl or large jug and leave it to cool at room temperature. Then cover it with cling film and place it in the refrigerator to chill for at least 1 hour.

Following the manufacturer's instructions, pour the chilled mixture into your ice cream maker and set it to churn. Once it has finished churning, decant the partially frozen ice cream into a freezer-friendly container and leave it in the freezer to set solid.

If you do not have an ice cream maker, follow the instructions on page 25.

Remove the ice cream from the freezer about 15 minutes before serving so that it can soften slightly.

# *birthday cake ice cream*

What would a birthday be without a large slice of sponge cake, jam oozing from between the layers and covered with a super-sweet marzipan coating? Well how about a scoop of birthday cake ice cream? To simulate the texture of sponge cake we use a pectin ice cream base, rather than a conventional custard-based one, and over-churn it to create the lightest and smoothest possible texture; almond extract suggests the marzipan, while a syringe full of raspberry jam provides the ice cream with a fruity jam filling.

1 sheet of pectin or gelatine (20–25g)
500ml double cream, preferably organic
1 tablespoon almond extract
2 egg yolks
150g vanilla sugar (see page 39)
400ml whole milk
2 tablespoons raspberry jam

Soak the pectin or gelatine sheet in a cup of cold water for 10 minutes, then remove and place in a saucepan with the milk. Simmer for five minutes over a medium heat, stirring almost constantly, until the pectin/gelatine is fully dissolved.

Reduce the heat to low. Add the cream and almond extract and vigorously whisk using a hand whisk to ensure that all of the ingredients are fully combined. Set the mixture aside to cool.

Meanwhile, in a mixing bowl, using a hand whisk or electric mixer, whisk together the egg yolks and vanilla sugar until they form a pale, smooth paste.

Whisk the egg paste into the milk mixture. Set aside for 30 minutes to allow the flavours to infuse and mature. Now whisk again for about 5 minutes to incorporate air into the mixture and so achieve a light texture.

Pour the mixture into a bowl or large jug. Cover it with cling film and place it in the refrigerator to chill for at least 1 hour.

Following the manufacturer's instructions, pour the chilled mixture into your ice cream maker and set it to churn. Once it has finished churning, decant the partially frozen ice cream into a freezer-friendly container. Re-whisk the mixture for a further 5 minutes and leave it in the freezer to set solid.

If you do not have an ice cream maker, follow the instructions on page 25.

Shortly before serving, remove the ice cream from the freezer and leave to soften for 5 minutes. Then scoop generous-sized balls on to a tray and, using a syringe, inject a small pool of raspberry jam into the centre of each ball. Return to the freezer until you are ready to serve.

# candied bacon and maple syrup ice cream

We originally created this recipe as a commission from the chefs at the Bristol-based Grillstock music and barbecue festival, who wanted a sweet, smoky, indulgent dessert for their menu. After we developed the recipe it came to be a favourite of mine. As an ice cream ingredient, candied bacon is sweet, complex and full of depth, with just a subtle meaty flavour that has something of a salted caramel dimension. Here we use a conventional French custard style of ice cream, over-churning the base mix to provide a silky-smooth, light texture.

5 rashers streaky bacon (smoked or unsmoked)
2 teaspoons light brown sugar
45g salted butter
140g brown sugar (light or dark)
1 teaspoon vanilla extract
650ml double cream
5 large free-range egg yolks
1 or 2 teaspoons dark rum or whisky
2 tablespoons maple syrup per serving, to serve

First prepare the bacon. Preheat the oven to 200°C/Gas Mark 6. Carefully lay the rashers of bacon on a baking sheet lined with kitchen foil, shiny side down.

Evenly sprinkle the brown sugar over each strip of bacon and bake for 7-8 minutes. Remove the tray from the oven and flip the bacon rashers over, dragging them through the dark, liquid sugar and fat which has collected on the baking tray. Return to the oven and continue to bake until the rashers have turned a very dark brown colour. Remove from oven and cool the rashers on a wire rack.

Once the rashers have cooled and solidified, roughly chop them into small pieces, no bigger than peanuts.

To make the ice cream base mix, melt the butter in a saucepan and gently stir in the brown sugar, vanilla extract and double cream. Sprinkle into the saucepan a small handful of the bacon pieces, submerging them in the cream to allow flavours to infuse. Bring to a simmer and leave simmering gently for 5 minutes. Remove from the heat.

Place the egg yolks in a mixing bowl. Add the warm brown sugar mixture, whisking constantly as you pour to create a smooth, thick paste.

Return the mixture to the saucepan. Add the rum or whisky and cook for about 10 minutes on a low-to-medium heat, stirring constantly to prevent it from curdling, until it has thickened enough to coat the back of the spoon. Remove from heat.

Pour the mixture into a bowl or large jug and leave it to cool at room temperature. Then cover it with cling film and place it in the refrigerator to chill for at least 1 hour.

Following the manufacturer's instructions, pour the chilled mixture into your ice cream maker and set it to churn. Add the remaining bacon pieces during the last moments of churning. Once it has finished churning, decant the partially frozen ice cream into a freezer-friendly container and leave it in the freezer to set solid.

If you do not have an ice cream maker, follow the instructions on page 25, adding the remaining bacon pieces just before placing the ice cream in the freezer for the first time.

Remove the ice cream from the freezer about 15 minutes before serving so that it can soften slightly.

Serve the ice cream in generous scoops topped with about 2 tablespoons of maple syrup per serving.

# liquid cheesecake ice cream

Flecked with digestive biscuit crust, this cheesecake ice cream is totally voluptuous. To suggest the soft, smooth texture of the original, this recipe uses pectin to thicken the base instead of egg yolks, as for the heavier French custard style of ice cream.

1 sheet of pectin or gelatine (20-25g)
350ml double cream
200ml whole milk
200g caster sugar
150g cream cheese
1 teaspoon vanilla extract
50g digestive biscuits, crushed

### for the fruit coulis

100g each of strawberries and raspberries, hulled
150g caster sugar

Soak the pectin or gelatine sheet in a cup of cold water for 10 minutes, then remove and place in a saucepan with the cream and milk. Simmer for five minutes over a medium heat, stirring almost constantly to avoid curdling the mixture, until the pectin/gelatine is fully dissolved. Remove the pan from the heat.

In a mixing bowl, whisk together the sugar, cream cheese and vanilla. Pour the hot milk mixture into the cream cheese mixture while whisking. Continue whisking until the ingredients are well combined.

Return the mixture to the heat and gently cook until it begins to thicken and form a velvety custard-like mixture; remember to stir almost constantly to prevent it from separating. When the mixture has thickened enough to coat the back of a spoon, remove from the heat, and set aside.

Pour the mixture into a bowl or large jug and leave it to cool at room temperature.

Then cover it with cling film and place it in the refrigerator to chill for at least 1 hour.

Following the manufacturer's instructions, pour the chilled mixture into your ice cream maker and set it to churn. When it starts to thicken, sprinkle in the crushed digestive biscuits, and restart the machine. When churning is complete, decant into a freezer-friendly container, gently whisk by hand for a few minutes, then place it in the freezer to set solid.

If you do not have an ice cream maker, follow the instructions on page 25, folding in the digestive biscuits when placing the ice cream in the freezer for the first time.

Meanwhile make the fruit coulis. First roughly chop the strawberries into small pieces. Gently heat them along with the raspberries in a saucepan over a medium heat for around 5 minutes, or until the fruit begins to break down.

Add the sugar and continue to cook the fruit for a further 5 minutes, or until the sugar has dissolved.

Remove the ice cream from the freezer about 15 minutes before serving so that it can soften slightly. Serve with the coulis poured over the top.

# vanilla ice cream cake

Often dismissed as 'plain' or 'boring', vanilla is actually a complex and recognisable flavour and hugely versatile, lending itself to many different pairings. For this recipe, rich Bourbon vanilla ice cream is combined with a light, soft sponge base and dark chocolate icing to create a real show stopper of an ice cream cake.

### for the sponge cake base
75g unsalted butter, softened
75g caster sugar
2 medium free-range eggs
75g self-raising flour
a little milk (optional)

### for the icing
200g dark chocolate (at least 70 percent
    cocoa solids)
100g unsalted butter

### for the Bourbon vanilla ice cream
1 vanilla pod
500ml double cream
400ml whole milk
180g caster sugar
6 large free-range egg yolks
1 tablespoon Madagascan vanilla extract

30g dark chocolate, grated, to decorate

First prepare the sponge cake base. Preheat the oven to 180°C/Gas Mark 4. Grease the sides of an 18cm/7in springform cake tin and line the base with baking parchment.

Using an electric hand mixer, cream the butter and caster sugar together until they form a thick, pale paste. Beat in the eggs, one at a time, then sift in the flour. Fold in the flour using a large spoon. At this stage the mixture should be of a thick, but malleable dropping consistency; if it is too thick, add a little milk.

Pour the mixture into the cake tin and gently spread out with a spatula to create an even surface. Bake for 25-30 minutes, or until an inserted skewer comes out clean. Place on a wire rack to cool completely.

Once the cake has cooled, remove the sides of the tin (but not the base); leave the cake on the wire rack.

Now prepare the icing. First temper the chocolate as instructed on page 111. Next, heat the chocolate and unsalted butter together in a bain marie (double boiler) until both have melted and thickened; set this aside to cool for 20 minutes.

Spread the icing thickly over the top and sides of the cake, so that it is fully encased. Leave the cake on the rack until the icing has hardened. Then place the cake on a large plate and replace the sides of the tin, but do not tighten them.

Using the recipe for Bourbon Vanilla Ice Cream (see page 48), mix up a full batch of ice cream and churn it in your ice cream maker. Once churning is complete and the ice cream is still soft, pour it into the cake tin on top of the cake, filling the tin to the brim. Even off the top with a palette knife or spatula. Place the cake in the freezer to set solid.

Remove the cake from the freezer and leave to soften for 10 minutes before removing the sides of the springform tin. Using a large spatula or cake slice, carefully remove the cake from the tin base and place it on another large plate to serve. Sprinkle the grated chocolate on top.

# *bourbon vanilla ice cream sandwich*

A generous helping of luxury vanilla ice cream carefully pressed between two moreish chocolate biscuits makes a simple, but sensuous treat. Vanilla is the classic choice, but you could, of course, substitute a different flavour of ice cream to create your own variation.

### *makes 6 (or more) sandwiches (with some ice cream left over)*

### *for the Bourbon vanilla ice cream*
1 vanilla pod
500ml double cream
400ml whole milk
180g caster sugar
6 large free-range egg yolks
1 tablespoon Madagascan vanilla extract

### *for the biscuits*
120g dark chocolate (at least 70 per cent cocoa solids)
120g unsalted butter, softened
50g caster sugar
100g light brown sugar
1 free-range egg
2 teaspoons vanilla extract
150g plain flour
1 teaspoon baking powder

First make the biscuits. Preheat the oven to 150°C/Gas Mark 2 and line a baking tray with baking parchment.

Temper the chocolate as instructed on page 111. When cool, roughly chop it into small pieces.

Place the butter, caster sugar and light brown sugar in a mixing bowl and, using an electric or hand whisk, beat them together until the mixture forms a smooth, pale paste. Then gradually beat in the egg and the vanilla extract.

In a separate mixing bowl stir the flour and baking powder together. Add this to the butter mixture, add the chocolate pieces and stir well to combine. The mixture should have a thick, stodgy consistency.

Lay a sheet of cling film on your worktop and scoop the dough into the middle. Using your hands, roll the mixture into an even cylinder, about 8–10cm in diameter, wrap it in cling film and place in the fridge for at least 1 hour to rest.

Remove the chilled dough from the fridge and slice into at least 12 discs. Place them on the baking tray and bake for at least 15 minutes, or until golden. Remove from the oven and set aside to cool.

Using the recipe for Bourbon Vanilla Ice Cream (see page 48), mix up a fresh batch of this ice cream. Once it has finished churning, but is not quite solid, scoop a ball into the middle of a biscuit and place another biscuit on top. Gently press the ice cream in place. (If you do not have an ice cream maker, follow the instructions on page 25, then allow the frozen ice cream to soften a little before assembling the sandwiches.)

Put the sandwiches into a sealable container and place them in the freezer to set solid before serving.

# *tutti frutti ice cream*

The Italian name of this colourful ice cream translates as 'all the fruits'. The ingredients vary, but they typically include glacé cherries and other candied fruits in a vanilla base. Why not experiment with your own favourite combination of fruits?

1 vanilla pod
300ml whole milk
300ml double cream
4 egg yolks
75g vanilla sugar (see page 39)
150g glacé cherries
150g mixed peel

Using a sharp knife, split the vanilla pod in half lengthways, then use the blunt edge of the knife to scrape out the seeds.

Pour the milk into a saucepan and add the vanilla pod and seeds. Cover the pan and place in the refrigerator for 24 hours to allow the flavours to infuse fully.

Remove the pan from the fridge and lift out the vanilla pod. Add the double cream, place the pan over a low heat and bring the mixture to a gentle simmer, stirring frequently to ensure that the mixture doesn't burn; do not allow it to boil. Let it simmer for about 5 minutes, then remove from the heat and set aside, remembering to stir occasionally.

Place the egg yolks and sugar in a mixing bowl and whisk together, using a hand or electric mixer, until you have a pale, thick and glossy paste.

Bring the milk mixture back up to a simmer, then gradually pour it into the egg mixture, whisking all the time, until it is well incorporated.

Return the mixture to the saucepan and cook for about 10 minutes on a low-to-medium heat, stirring constantly, to prevent it from curdling, until it has thickened enough to coat the back of the spoon. Remove from heat.

Pour the mixture into a bowl or large jug and leave it to cool at room temperature. Then cover it with cling film and place it in the refrigerator to chill for at least 1 hour.

Following the manufacturer's instructions, pour the chilled mixture into your ice cream maker and set it to churn. When it has finished churning, or the ice cream is well thickened, add the fruit and re-set to churn for a further 10 minutes. Decant the partially frozen ice cream into a freezer-friendly container and leave it in the freezer to set solid.

If you do not have an ice cream maker, follow the instructions on page 25.

Remove the ice cream from the freezer about 15 minutes before serving so that it can soften slightly.

# *vanilla and espresso affogato*

In Italian affogato literally means 'drowned'. Here it denotes ice cream, served in a shallow bowl or coffee cup along with an amaretto-laced coffee granita, 'drowning' in a steaming hot shot of espresso – teasing the palate with the contrast between piping hot and ice cold.

*makes 3–5 servings*

*for the Bourbon vanilla ice cream*
1 vanilla pod
500ml double cream
400ml whole milk
180g caster sugar
6 large free-range egg yolks
1 tablespoon Madagascan vanilla extract

*for the espresso granita*
2 tablespoons vanilla sugar (see page 39)
1 shot of hot espresso or other strong brewed
    coffee
25ml good-quality amaretto liqueur

*to serve*
200ml steaming hot espresso or other strong
    black coffee

Following the recipe on page 48, make a batch of Bourbon Vanilla Ice Cream. Leave it in the freezer until required.

Now make the granita. Place the vanilla sugar in a dish and pour a shot of boiling-hot espresso or other strong coffee over it. Stir until the sugar is fully dissolved, then stir in the amaretto. Decant into a freezer-friendly container and place in the freezer to set solid.

Remove the ice cream from the freezer 15 minutes before serving to soften slightly. Make the coffee. Place a spoonful of the granita in a shallow glass, top with a generous scoop of ice cream and then pour over a little of the steaming hot coffee.

# baked alaska

Said to have been invented by a New York chef in the late-nineteenth century, Baked Alaska is a pudding mountain of ice cream and meringue set on a bed of sponge cake and really is something to behold. The meringue coating, cooked as briefly as possible, acts as insulation for the ice cream. This version, made with vanilla ice cream, is enlivened with a layer of raspberry jam and 'cheats' by using a ready-made sponge cake. Alternatively, you could use Christmas pudding or Madeira cake as a base.

### for the Bourbon vanilla ice cream
1 vanilla pod
500ml double cream
400ml whole milk
180g caster sugar
6 large free-range egg yolks
1 tablespoon Madagascan vanilla extract

### for the meringue
3 free-range egg whites
175g/6oz vanilla sugar (see page 39)

### to assemble
1 thick sponge cake, at least 20cm in
    diameter/width
3 tablespoons raspberry jam

Following the recipe on page 48, make a batch of Bourbon Vanilla Ice Cream. Leave it in the freezer until required.

Now make the meringue. Whisk the egg whites in a large, clean mixing bowl (any trace of grease will inhibit the volume) until stiff peaks begin to form. Slowly add the vanilla sugar, whisking well after each addition. Continue to whisk until glossy, velvety-smooth and very stiff peaks form.

Preheat the oven to 200°C/Gas Mark 6.

Assemble the Alaska just before you plan to serve it. Cut the sponge cake into a round, 20-25cm in diameter. Thickly spread the jam over the cake, then arrange scoops of ice cream in a towering pyramid shape on top, leaving a small border of sponge around the edges. Generously spoon the meringue all over the ice cream, ensuring that there are no gaps, and use the back of a spoon to make a rough swirl pattern.

Bake the Alaska for 8–10 minutes, or until golden-brown all over. Or finish by toasting the outside with a cook's blowtorch until golden.

# *classic banana split*

The darling of the American soda fountain, the banana split was invented in the early 1900s and remains the ultimate ice cream indulgence. The original, classic version includes three scoops of ice cream, vanilla, chocolate and strawberry, each with its own topping, sprinkled with chopped nuts and surmounted with whipped cream and a maraschino cherry. Our chocolate-and-vanilla version, smothered in toffee syrup and whipped cream is equally wicked. Go on, treat yourself!

*makes 4 servings (with some ice cream left over)*

*for the Bourbon vanilla ice cream*
1 vanilla pod
500ml double cream
400ml whole milk
180g caster sugar
6 large free-range egg yolks
1 tablespoon Madagascan vanilla extract

*for the chocolate ice cream*
300ml double cream
200ml whole milk
100g dark muscovado sugar
200g dark chocolate (at least 75 per cent
   cocoa solids)
75g caster sugar
4 large, free-range egg yolks

*to assemble*
1 rounded teaspoon caster sugar
250ml whipping cream
4 large ripe bananas
a few tablespoons toffee syrup (page 95)
5 tablespoons crushed nuts, such as peanuts
   or walnuts
10 glacé cherries, halved

Make a batch of Bourbon Vanilla Ice Cream and Chocolate Ice Cream, following the recipes on pages 48 and 126 respectively. Place them in the freezer to set solid and leave until required.

Add the caster sugar to the whipping cream and whip until it forms fairly stiff peaks.

Carefully peel the bananas, slice them in half lengthways and place two halves in each of 4 boat-shaped dishes.

Place 2 scoops of vanilla and 2 of chocolate ice cream down the length of each banana, between the two halves. Drizzle generously with toffee syrup over the top.

Generously spoon whipped cream over the ice cream. Sprinkle liberally with chopped nuts and top with glacé cherries and serve straight away.

# bananas foster

Invented in 1951 in New Orleans by a chef at Brennan's Restaurant and named for a favourite patron, this is a luscious and impressive dessert.

### for the banana sauce

50g butter, softened
120g light brown sugar
$\frac{1}{2}$ teaspoon ground nutmeg
1 teaspoon ground cinnamon
4 tablespoons banana liqueur
4 bananas, peeled and sliced lengthways and
    crossways, to make 4 quarters
4 tablespoons light rum
150ml whipping cream
2 teaspoons caster sugar or cinnamon
    (optional)

### for the Bourbon vanilla ice cream

1 vanilla pod
500ml double cream
400ml whole milk
180g caster sugar
6 large free-range egg yolks
1 tablespoon Madagascan vanilla extract

Make a batch of Bourbon Vanilla Ice Cream following the recipe on page 48; leave it in the freezer until required.

Place the butter, sugar, nutmeg and cinnamon in a frying pan and cook slowly over a medium heat until the sugar has melted.

Stir in the banana liqueur, then add the banana pieces and cook, stirring carefully, until the bananas have absorbed some of the syrup and have begun to soften, turning a rich golden brown.

Add the light rum and gently stir to combine. Turn up the heat and carefully flambé the rum – either (gas hob) by moving the pan towards you and tilting it away from you, so that the gas at the far edge ignites the alcohol, or by using a candle lighter. In either case, stand well back to avoid burning yourself. Leave the pan on heat until the flames die out.

If desired, add 2 teaspoons caster sugar or cinnamon to the whipping cream, for extra sweetness/spiciness. Whip the cream using an electric mixer until it forms soft peaks.

To serve, place a scoop of ice cream in a shallow glass dish, top with the banana pieces, add a dollop of whipped cream, and pour the sauce from the pan on top.

# *moondust frozen yoghurt*

A subtle hint of vanilla paired with rum, some crunchy toasted almonds, and a sprinkling of silver glitter help to make this delectable frozen yoghurt a dessert that's virtually out of this world.

500g Greek yoghurt
2 teaspoons vanilla extract
2 teaspoons light rum
225g caster sugar
2 teaspoons lemon juice
2 teaspoons edible silver glitter
2 teaspoons toasted flaked almonds

Place the Greek yoghurt in a saucepan, stir in the vanilla and rum, and cook over a low heat for 5 minutes, stirring regularly.

Remove the pan from the heat and gently stir in the caster sugar and lemon juice. Ensure they are well mixed in, then place the pan back over a low heat for a further 5 minutes to dissolve the sugar. Remove the pan from the heat.

Pour the mixture into a bowl or large jug and set aside to cool. Once cool, pour the glitter and toasted almonds into the yoghurt. Using a fork or a hand whisk, mix the glitter and almonds consistently throughout the yoghurt. Place in the fridge to chill for 1 hour.

Pour the chilled mixture into your ice cream maker and set it to churn. Once it has finished churning, decant the partially frozen yoghurt into a freezer-friendly container and leave it in the freezer to set solid.

If you do not have an ice cream maker, follow the instructions on page 25.

Remove the frozen yoghurt from the freezer about 15 minutes before serving so that it can soften slightly.

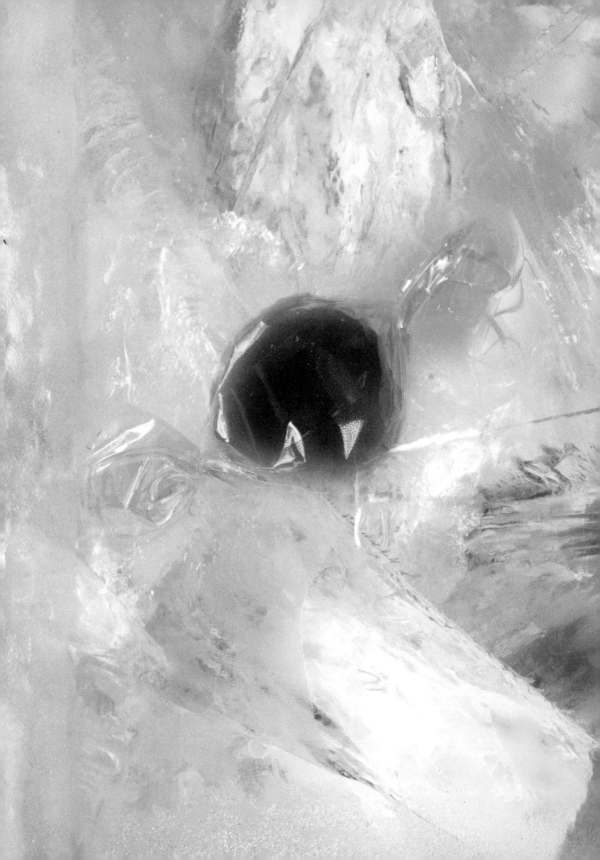

sugar,
caramel and
toffee

By cooking sugar until it caramelises we can create wonderful flavours and inclusions for ice cream. These include toffee and butterscotch and caramel itself. All of these are similar in taste (although caramel in its pure form is bittersweet, rather than sweet like the others), differing mainly in texture, with caramel being soft, butterscotch crisp and brittle, and toffee varying degrees of chewy, from soft to hard.

The process of caramelisation is scientifically complex, but essentially caramel is produced at the final stage of boiling sugar, when it reaches a temperature of about 160–170°C. (This applies to sucrose, or white sugar. Some forms of sugar, such as fructose, or fruit sugar, found in honey for example, caramelise at lower temperatures.) At this point the sugar is degraded and changed into many different compounds; however, if heating exceeds 170°C for a sustained period the syrup will burn and become too bitter. Constant attention and a sugar thermometer are crucial when making caramel.

## Brown sugar

Until the nineteenth century people ate unrefined sugar, called 'raw sugar', which was brown in colour. Then a method of extracting the molasses from this sugar was developed, to produce the refined white sugar used for most purposes today. The molasses, a syrupy brown liquid, is used in a broad range of foodstuffs and in some cookery. Today, brown sugar of various kinds, including muscovado and demerara, is valued for its rich taste; ironically, most of the brown sugar we eat today is produced by adding molasses to refined white sugar – putting back what we take out. Brown sugar is often used to make caramel, butterscotch and toffee, as it gives an extra richness to the mixture, and I have used it in most of the recipes in this chapter. An alternative is to use white sugar and treacle to intensify the flavour.

## Salted caramel

Thought to have originated in Brittany in the 1970s, salted caramel is the darling of the confectionery world right now. This is a delicious blend of brown sugar, butter, cream, golden syrup and coarse sea salt. To make a salted caramel topping sauce for ice cream, simply melt 100g of salted butter in a pan for several minutes, then add 125ml double cream and $1/2$ tablespoon coarse sea salt, 100g light brown sugar and 50g golden syrup.

Continue to heat for about 10 minutes, stirring occasionally, then set it aside to cool. Once cool, transfer the sauce to a container with a lid and place in the refrigerator. The sauce can be used either cold or warm – gently reheated in the microwave or on the hob.

## Hard toffee

You can easily make toffee at home, with the help of a sugar thermometer. Here is a recipe for the hard stuff (mind your teeth!). First grease a shallow baking tin with a knob of butter. Place 200g of light brown sugar, 250g of golden syrup and 2 tablespoons of vinegar in a saucepan and cook over a low heat, stirring frequently, until the sugar is dissolved. Increase the heat to medium and cook until a sugar thermometer reads 120°C, remembering to keep stirring. Add to the pan 200g of dark treacle and 30g of butter and continue to cook, stirring occasionally, until the sugar thermometer reads 120–130°C. (This is called the 'hard crack' stage: a small amount of the hot mixture, if dropped into a bowl of cold water, will solidify and harden, forming brittle threads.) Remove from the heat. Add $1/_2$ teaspoon of bicarbonate of soda and mix well. Finally, pour the mixture into the prepared tin and allow it to rest until hardened. Roughly break off bits of toffee (a toffee hammer is useful for this) and store in an airtight container.

## Soft toffee

To create soft toffee, prepare the tin as for hard toffee. Place 120g of salted butter in a saucepan along with 3 tablespoons of dark treacle, 3 tablespoons of whole milk and 6 tablespoons of granulated sugar. Quickly bring the mixture to a boil, then remove from the heat for a couple of minutes, return to the heat and continue to boil for 20 minutes, or until the mixture reaches 110–115°C. (This is the 'soft ball' stage: a small amount of the mixture dropped into cold water forms a soft, malleable ball.) Pour the mixture into the tin and leave it to set. When it's nearly solid, mark it into squares of about 2.5cm; break it up when it has cooled completely.

# *banoffee pie*

Invented in 1972 at the Hungry Monk Restaurant (now unfortunately closed) in East Sussex, banoffee pie takes its inspiration from a traditional American coffee toffee pie. The original banoffee pie was constructed using condensed milk, cream, bananas and sugar, and so, too, in staying true to its origins, is this ice cream.

4 ripe bananas, cut into small chunks
25g butter, at room temperature
75g light brown sugar
250g condensed milk
350ml double cream
1 teaspoon ground cinnamon
100g digestive biscuits, crushed

Preheat the oven to 200°C/Gas Mark 6. Place the banana chunks in a ceramic casserole or baking dish, cover with the butter and sugar, and bake for 25–30 minutes. Remove from the oven and set aside to cool.

Transfer the bananas to a blender or food processor and blend for 5 minutes, or until the mixture is completely puréed.

Meanwhile, gently heat the condensed milk in a small pan until it becomes runny. Remove from the heat and set aside to cool slightly, then pour it into a mixing bowl and add the double cream. Whisk the mixture until it begins to thicken and form soft peaks.

Now stir the banana purée, the cinnamon and the crushed biscuits. Once well mixed, place in the fridge to chill for 1 hour.

Pour the chilled mixture into your ice cream maker and set it to churn. Once it has finished churning, decant the partially frozen ice cream into a freezer-friendly container and leave it in the freezer to set solid.

If you do not have an ice cream maker, follow the instructions on page 25.

Remove the ice cream from the freezer about 15 minutes before serving so that it can soften slightly.

# *butterscotch chip ice cream*

This rich ice cream has a French (custard) ice cream base, made using light brown muscovado sugar, which enhances and complements the shards of butterscotch stirred into it and sprinkled on top.

### *For the butterscotch chips*
350g demerara sugar
150ml water
1 teaspoon white vinegar
120g unsalted butter
4 tablespoons double cream

### *For the ice cream base*
100g butter, softened
100g light brown muscovado sugar
200ml double cream
350ml whole milk
3 large free-range egg yolks

First make the butterscotch. Line a baking tray with kitchen foil. Place the demerara sugar and water in a saucepan and gently cook over a medium heat, stirring constantly, until the sugar has dissolved. Stop stirring, add the vinegar and bring to the boil (135–140°C). Immediately turn off the heat and stir in the butter and cream.

While the mixture is still piping hot, pour it into the foil-lined tray, score into 5 or 6 narrow rows and leave to set solid. Once solid, break it into small shards using a toffee hammer, or cover with a tea towel and strike it with a rolling pin.

Next make the ice cream base. Place the softened butter, sugar, cream, milk and 2 tablespoons water in a saucepan over a low-to-medium heat and bring to a simmer, stirring frequently to ensure that the mixture doesn't burn; do not allow it to boil. Let it simmer for 10 minutes, then remove from heat and set aside, remembering to stir occasionally.

In a mixing bowl whisk the egg yolks until light and fluffy.

Bring the milk mixture back up to a simmer, then gradually pour it into the egg mixture, whisking all the time, until it is well incorporated.

Return the mixture to the saucepan and cook for about 10 minutes on a low-to-medium heat, stirring constantly, until it has thickened enough to coat the back of the spoon. Remove from heat.

Pour the mixture into a bowl or large jug and leave it to cool at room temperature. Then cover it with cling film and place it in the refrigerator to chill for at least 1 hour.

Pour the chilled mixture into your ice cream maker, along with a handful of the butterscotch chips, and set it to churn. Once it has finished churning, decant the partially frozen ice cream into a freezer-friendly container and leave it in the freezer to set solid.

If you do not have an ice cream maker, follow the instructions on page 25, adding the butterscotch chips before placing in the freezer for the first time.

Remove the ice cream from the freezer about 15 minutes before serving so that it can soften slightly.

To serve, decorate the ice cream with the remaining butterscotch chips.

# brown bread ice cream

Brown bread makes for a uniquely nutty, moreish ice cream, packed full of sweet caramel-flavour notes. A classic recipe from Victorian times, when ice cream was beginning to become hugely popular, it uses a French custard base, brown sugar and vanilla extract.

### for the caramelised breadcrumbs
50g salted butter
150g brown bread, crusts removed and
    roughly diced
150g light brown sugar, plus a little extra
1 teaspoon ground cinnamon
1 teaspoon mixed spice

### for the ice cream base
250ml whole milk
350ml double cream
5 free-range egg yolks
150g light brown sugar
1 teaspoon vanilla extract
a dash of lemon juice
1 teaspoon white rum

Begin by making the caramelised breadcrumbs. Preheat the oven to 180°C/Gas Mark 4. Heat the butter in a pan over a medium heat until it melts and then begins to brown. Remove from the heat and add the diced bread, sugar and spices, stirring to ensure that all ingredients are fully combined. Set aside to cool.

Spread the cooled mixture out on a baking tray, top with an extra sprinkling of brown sugar and bake for 25 minutes until golden brown. Remove from the oven and leave to cool, then break up using a fork and set aside.

Now make the ice cream base. Pour the milk and cream into a saucepan and place over a low-to-medium heat. Bring to a simmer, stirring frequently to ensure that the mixture doesn't burn; do not allow it to boil. Let it simmer for about 5 minutes, then remove from the heat and set aside, remembering to stir occasionally.

Place the egg yolks and sugar in a mixing bowl and whisk together until you have a pale, thick and glossy paste.

Bring the milk mixture back up to a simmer, then gradually pour it into the egg mixture, whisking all the time, until it is well incorporated.

Return the mixture to the saucepan and add the vanilla, lemon juice and rum. Cook for about 10 minutes on a low-to-medium heat, stirring constantly, until it has thickened enough to coat the back of the spoon. Remove from heat.

Pour the mixture into a bowl or large jug and stir in about half of the caramelised brown breadcrumbs. Leave the mixture to cool at room temperature, then cover it with cling film and place it in the refrigerator to chill for at least 1 hour.

Pour the chilled mixture into your ice cream maker and set it to churn. Once it has finished churning, stir in the remaining caramelised brown breadcrumbs, decant the partially frozen ice cream into a freezer-friendly container and leave it in the freezer to set solid.

If you do not have an ice cream maker, follow the instructions on page 25, adding the remaining breadcrumbs before placing it in the freezer for the first time.

Remove the ice cream from the freezer about 15 minutes before serving so that it can soften slightly.

# salted caramel ice cream

Flecked with the mildly bitter and dry taste of coarse sea salt and shards of freshly made salted caramel, this ice cream recipe oozes style and panache and is simple enough to make within just a couple of hours from start to scoop.

### for the caramel inclusions
100g caster sugar
1 tablespoon coarse sea salt

### for the ice cream base
500ml whole milk
250ml double cream
5 large free-range egg yolks
300g caster sugar
50g salted butter
1 teaspoon sea salt

Begin by making the caramel inclusions. First line a baking tray with kitchen foil. Pour the sugar into a saucepan and heat it over a medium heat for around 5–10 minutes, stirring constantly and using a thermometer to monitor the temperature of the liquefying sugar.

When the sugar reaches 160°C remove from the heat, mix in the salt and pour the mixture on to the foil-lined baking tray. Set aside to cool and allow the caramel to harden off. Then roughly break it into small shards, using a toffee hammer; or cover it with a tea towel and strike with a rolling pin.

Now make the ice cream base. Pour the milk and cream into a saucepan and place over a low-to-medium heat. Bring to a simmer, stirring frequently to ensure that the mixture doesn't burn; do not allow it to boil. Let it simmer for about 5 minutes, then remove from the heat and set aside, remembering to stir occasionally.

Place the egg yolks and sugar in a mixing bowl and whisk together until you have a pale, thick and glossy paste.

Bring the milk mixture back up to a simmer, then gradually pour it into the egg mixture, whisking all the time, until it is well incorporated.

Return the mixture to the saucepan and add the butter and salt. Cook for about 10 minutes on a low-to-medium heat, stirring constantly, until it has thickened enough to coat the back of the spoon. Remove from heat.

When the mixture has cooled a little, pour it into a bowl or large jug, stir in about half of the caramel shards and leave to infuse. Once the mixture has cooled to room temperature, cover it with cling film and place it in the refrigerator to chill for at least 1 hour.

Pour the chilled mixture into your ice cream maker and set it to churn. Once it has finished churning, decant the partially frozen ice cream into a freezer-friendly container, add the remaining caramel shards, and leave it in the freezer to set solid.

If you do not have an ice cream maker, follow the instructions on page 25, adding the remaining caramel shards before placing it in the freezer for the first time.

Remove the ice cream from the freezer about 15 minutes before serving so that it can soften slightly.

# toffee fudge ice cream

The taste of fudge takes me straight back to my annual summer holidays in Dorset with my parents and brother, sitting on the beach in picturesque Swanage, chomping away on fudge, while the waves lapped up against the sea wall. It's a quintessentially British flavour which derives from brown sugar and lots of it.

### for the fudge inclusions
150ml whole milk
150g light brown sugar
50g unsalted butter

### for the ice cream base
500ml whole milk
250ml double cream
1 tablespoon thick clotted cream
5 large free-range egg yolks
150g light brown sugar
25g unsalted butter, softened

First make the fudge inclusions. Line a baking tray with kitchen foil. Place the milk, sugar and butter in a saucepan over a medium heat and cook gently, stirring almost constantly to stop the mixture from burning. Continue to heat until the sugar has fully dissolved and the butter melted and the ingredients are fully combined.

Now bring the mixture to the boil and boil for about 15 minutes, stirring constantly and using a sugar thermometer to check the temperature. When the mixture reaches 115°C (the soft-ball stage) remove it from the heat and set aside to cool for about 10 minutes.

Pour the mixture into the baking tray and score into a grid pattern, placing the lines about 2–3cm apart. Leave to set solid.

Now make the ice cream base. Pour the milk and cream into a saucepan and place over a low-to-medium heat. Bring to a simmer, stirring frequently to ensure that the mixture doesn't burn; do not allow it to boil.

Let it simmer for about 5 minutes, then add the clotted cream; stir to combine fully. Remove from the heat and set aside, remembering to stir occasionally.

Place the egg yolks and sugar in a mixing bowl and whisk together until you have a pale, thick and glossy paste.

Bring the milk mixture back up to a simmer, then gradually pour it into the egg mixture, whisking all the time, until it is well incorporated.

Return the mixture to the saucepan and place over a low heat. Gently increase the heat to bring the mixture close to the boiling point and continue cooking stirring constantly, for 10 minutes; stir in the butter and immediately remove from the heat.

Pour the mixture into a bowl or large jug and leave it to cool at room temperature. Then cover it with cling film and place it in the refrigerator to chill for at least 1 hour.

Remove the chilled mixture from the fridge and whisk vigorously to aerate the mixture and ensure the ingredients have combined fully.

Roughly chop up the fudge pieces to about the size of peanuts, using a toffee hammer; or cover with a tea towel and strike with a rolling pin. Fold them into the aerated ice cream.

Pour the mixture into your ice cream maker and set it to churn. Once it has finished churning, decant the partially frozen ice cream into a freezer-friendly container and leave it in the freezer to set solid.

If you do not have an ice cream maker, follow the instructions on page 25.

Remove the ice cream from the freezer about 15 minutes before serving so that it can soften slightly.

# *toffee fudge sundae*

Ithaca, New York, is generally accepted as the birthplace of the ice cream sundae – named (with a little tweak of the spelling) after the Sunday, in 1892, when it was created. That first sundae consisted of vanilla ice cream topped with cherry syrup and a candied cherry. Since then, sundaes have included many different ice cream flavours and toppings. This one combines two flavours of ice cream: Bourbon Vanilla and a deconstructed version of Toffee Fudge Ice Cream, with the toffee pieces added separately for extra impact. A rich toffee syrup, some chopped pecans /walnuts and a helping of whipped cream add yet more excitement.

### *makes 3 sundaes*

### *for the toffee syrup*
80g light brown sugar
50g dark brown sugar
200ml double cream
50g unsalted butter
1 tablespoon golden syrup

### *for the toffee fudge*
150ml whole milk
150g light brown sugar
50g unsalted butter

### *for the toffee ice cream*
500ml whole milk
150g light brown sugar
250ml double cream
5 large free-range egg yolks

### *for the Bourbon vanilla ice cream*
1 vanilla pod
500ml double cream
400ml whole milk
180g caster sugar
6 large free-range egg yolks
1 tablespoon Madagascan vanilla extract

### *for the topping*
150ml whipping cream
1 teaspoon caster sugar
3–5 tablespoons chopped pecans

First make the toffee syrup. Pour all of the ingredients into a saucepan over a low heat and whisk until the butter has melted, the sugar has dissolved and all of the ingredients are fully combined into a smooth, thick syrup. Leave the sauce to cool, then place in the fridge to chill until needed.

Using the recipe on page 92, make a batch of toffee fudge. Set aside.

Using the recipes on pages 48 and 92 respectively, make a fresh batch each of Bourbon Vanilla and Toffee Fudge ice cream (omitting the fudge, already made). When each ice cream has finished churning, decant it into a separate freezer-friendly container and leave them in the freezer to set solid.

When nearly ready to serve, whip the cream (including the caster sugar) to form soft peaks.

Line 3 sundae glasses with toffee syrup, turning the glass to coat the inner surface, and fill the bottom of the glass with a handful of roughly cut fudge, followed by a generous helping of toffee syrup. Add the two ice creams alternately. To finish in decadent fashion, top with more toffee syrup and chopped nuts and the whipped cream. Serve with long sundae spoons.

# saffron and caramel kulfi

Kulfi is a traditional Indian dessert similar to ice cream, made using sweetened condensed milk. Unlike traditional Western ice cream, it is made without the addition of air, so is thick, dense and rich, thanks to the slow-cooked caramelisation of the ingredients. Once cooked and partially frozen, kulfi is traditionally poured into moulds and frozen for up to 24 hours, then served with a garnish of cardamom pods and toasted pistachio nuts.

### makes 4 medium-sized kulfi servings

$1/_2$ teaspoon cornflour
300ml condensed milk
200ml double cream
100g light brown sugar
1 teaspoon saffron threads
2 teaspoons golden syrup

### to serve
100g pistachio nuts, toasted
4 whole cardamom pods

Mix the cornflour with the condensed milk in a saucepan and place over a low-to-medium heat, then bring to a rapid simmer, stirring constantly.

Add the double cream, sugar, saffron and golden syrup and stir well, using a hand whisk, to ensure all of the ingredients are well combined. Continue to heat until all of the sugar has dissolved. Remove the pan from the heat and set aside to cool.

Once cool, beat the mixture with an electric whisk for a couple of minutes at high speed to ensure that there are absolutely no lumps in it – a common occurrence when using condensed milk.

Pour the mixture into a large jug, cover with cling film and place in the fridge to chill for 1 hour.

Pour the chilled mixture into your ice cream maker and set it to churn. Once it has finished churning, decant the partially frozen kulfi into your kulfi moulds (or jelly or ice lolly moulds) and place these in the freezer to set solid.

Unmould the kulfi on to dessert plates and sprinkle the toasted pistachios and a cardamom pod on top of each.

# dulce de leche mascarpone ice cream

An absolute favourite which I discovered at a backstreet ice cream parlour while holidaying in Venice, Dulce de Leche and Mascarpone Ice Cream is devilishly delicious, smooth and creamy. Thought to have originated in Argentina, *dulce de leche* (Spanish) translates as 'sweet [or candy] of milk' or 'milk jam'.
To achieve a thick, creamy dulce de leche we slowly heat sweetened condensed milk to caramelise its sugar content. The mascarpone adds even more richness and a topping of toasted pecans provides the perfect finishing touch.

300ml sweetened condensed milk
250ml whole milk
250ml double cream
1 teaspoon ground cinnamon
50g mascarpone
a pinch of salt

### to serve
50g chopped and toasted pecans

Pour the condensed milk into a saucepan and cook over a medium heat, stirring frequently until it becomes thick and glossy and a golden caramel colour. This will take quite a long time, about 1 hour.

In another saucepan bring the whole milk and cream to a simmer; stir in the cinnamon, mascarpone and salt. Stir frequently to prevent the milk from burning. Reduce the heat and gradually whisk in the condensed milk until fully combined.

Remove the mixture from the heat, pour it into a bowl or large jug and set aside to cool. Once cool, cover the mixture with cling film and set in the refrigerator to chill for 1 hour.

Meanwhile, scatter the chopped pecans over a baking tray and toast in the oven at 150°C/Gas Mark 2 for 20 minutes. Set aside to cool for use later on.

Remove the chilled ice cream from the fridge and give it a good whisking for a few minutes to ensure smoothness and incorporate a little air.

Pour the mixture into your ice cream maker and set it to churn. Once it has finished churning, stir in the toasted pecans, decant the partially frozen ice cream into a freezer-friendly container and leave it in the freezer to set solid.

If you do not have an ice cream maker, follow the instructions on page 25, stirring in the toasted pecans before placing the ice cream in the freezer for the first time.

Remove the ice cream from the freezer about 15 minutes before serving so that it can soften slightly.

# golden syrup crunch ice cream

When the sugar manufacturer Abram Lyle noticed, in 1883, that a gloopy golden syrup was produced in the refining process, he quickly saw its potential. With further refining, his 'Golden Syrup' was launched to much success and, since then, the green and gold tins have become truly iconic. By replacing sugar with golden syrup and adding this to milk, cream, egg yolks and vanilla extract, you can easily create a very simple and delicious ice cream.

4 free-range egg yolks
150g golden syrup
250ml whole milk
1 teaspoon vanilla extract
250ml double cream

Using an electric whisk, beat the egg yolks in a mixing bowl for about 5 minutes, until the yolks become a pale, smooth paste. Pour this into a saucepan and gently warm on a low heat, stirring the mixture constantly to avoid burning it.

Remove the pan from the heat. Carefully fold the golden syrup into the egg mixture along with the milk, vanilla and cream.

Return the mixture to heat, and continue to stir until the ingredients are fully combined and the mixture is thick enough to coat the back of a spoon. Remove from heat, pour into a bowl or large jug and set aside to cool.

Once cool, cover the mixture with cling film and place it in the fridge to chill for at least 1 hour. Then remove and whisk it vigorously to aerate the mixture.

Pour the ice cream mixture into your ice cream maker and set it to churn. Once it has finished churning, decant the partially frozen ice cream into a freezer-friendly container and leave it in the freezer to set solid.

If you do not have an ice cream maker, follow the instructions on page 25.

Remove the ice cream from the freezer about 15 minutes before serving so that it can soften slightly. Immediately drizzle golden syrup over the ice cream – it will become hard and crunchy.

# *maple syrup gelato*

Softer than ice cream, commercial gelato contains very little air and thus is relatively dense, with a silky-smooth texture. Importantly, to stabilise the mixture, gelato also often contains – in place of air – a higher number of egg yolks than ice cream. The use of maple syrup in this gelato produces a frozen dessert with a voluptuous flavour and texture reminiscent of runny honey.

500ml double cream
400ml whole milk
60ml maple syrup
6 large free-range egg yolks
100g caster sugar

Pour the cream and milk into a saucepan, tip in half the sugar and briefly whisk to combine. Place over a low heat for 3–5 minutes, stirring frequently to ensure that the mixture doesn't burn; do not allow it to boil. Now mix in the maple syrup; bring the mixture to a simmer and leave it to bubble gently for 10 minutes. Remove from the heat and set aside, remembering to stir occasionally.

Place the egg yolks and sugar in a mixing bowl and whisk together until you have a pale, thick and glossy paste.

Bring the milk mixture back up to a simmer, then gradually pour it into the egg mixture, whisking all the time, until it is well incorporated.

Return the mixture to the saucepan and cook for about 10 minutes on a low-to-medium heat, stirring constantly, until it has thickened enough to coat the back of the spoon. Remove from heat.

Pour the mixture into a bowl or large jug and leave it to cool at room temperature. Then cover it with cling film and place it in the refrigerator to chill for at least 1 hour. This will also give the maple syrup time to fully infuse and mature.

Pour the chilled mixture into your ice cream maker and set it to churn. Once it has finished churning, decant the partially frozen ice cream into a freezer-friendly container and leave it in the freezer to set solid.

If you do not have an ice cream maker, follow the instructions on page 25.

Remove the ice cream from the freezer about 15 minutes before serving so that it can soften slightly.

# coke float

Dating back to the American soda fountain craze of the early to mid-twentieth century, and popularised during the 1950s, when soda fountains were at the centre of teenage subculture, the Coke float is a simple, sweet combination of cola, vanilla ice cream and vanilla extract. For children and young-at-heart adults alike, it's heaven in a glass!

*makes 6 drinks*

*for the Bourbon vanilla ice cream*
500ml double cream
400ml whole milk
1 vanilla pod
180g caster sugar
6 large free-range egg yolks
1 tablespoon Madagascan vanilla extract

*to create the float*
3 teaspoons vanilla extract
6 glacé cherries
2.5 litres cola

Using the recipe for Bourbon Vanilla Ice Cream (see page 48), mix up a batch of ice cream. Place it in the freezer until ready to scoop.

When the ice cream is set, place 6 tall glasses in the freezer for 5 minutes to frost.

Place one or two scoops of ice cream in the bottom of each glass, then pour half a teaspoon of vanilla extract over the top and swirl carefully to ensure the scoop is evenly coated. Fill the glass with cola and serve with a long straw and a sundae spoon to get the last mouthfuls of ice cream. A nice extra touch is to serve with a glacé cherry.

# cherry cola ice lollies

The brown sugar base of this recipe, along with the caramel flavour notes found in cola, produces a distinct flavour of toffee, which offsets the sour fruitiness of cherry juice. Try using different kinds of cherry juice to vary the flavour. The recipe can be used for either ice lollies or ice cubes.

*makes 15 ice lollies or 20 ice cubes*

500ml cola drink
125g light brown sugar
2 tablespoons cherry juice

Pour half of the cola into a small saucepan and bring to a rapid boil; continue boiling for 15 minutes to allow the liquid to reduce by 50 per cent. Then remove from the heat and set aside to cool.

Stir in the sugar and cherry juice, return the pan to a medium heat and pour in the remaining cola. Bring to a simmer, stirring constantly to help the sugar dissolve and to stop the mixture from burning. Continue to heat for 5 more minutes, then remove from the heat and set aside to cool.

Pour the cooled mixture into lolly moulds or ice cube trays. If using moulds, allow a 1cm clearance at the top to allow for a small amount of expansion. Place the lollies/ice cubes in the freezer to set solid.

chocolate

*choco*

Native to Mexico and Central America, chocolate was first brought to Europe in the 16th century by Spanish explorers and conquistadors, notably Hernán Cortés, conqueror of Mexico. They found the seeds of the cacao tree being used by the Aztecs to make a drink and also in various foods and medicines. By the eighteenth century chocolate had become a highly fashionable hot drink enjoyed by the nobility and the rich bourgeoisie. It was not until the early nineteenth century that a method of producing eating chocolate was invented.

Chocolate is one of the best-loved types of confectionery and my own personal favourite. In sweetened form, it has a quality of innocence and nostalgia for people of all ages. But its effect is far more complex than this would suggest. Chocolate is a chemically perfect treat, containing anandamide, which helps the brain to release endorphins: proteins that produce a feeling of well-being. Chocolate is also packed full of antioxidants.

The processing and ingredients that go into chocolate can create a vast array of flavours, from nutty and earthy to bitter or overtly sweet. Similarly the different techniques of chocolate processing and tempering can produce a wide variety of textures which alter our perception and enjoyment of the finished product.

Chocolate marries beautifully with many fruits, herbs and spices, including citrus fruits such as oranges, mandarins and limes; cherries; rosemary; and even chilli. Some of these are featured in the following recipes.

## Manufacturing chocolate

In Western Europe chocolate has been commercially manufactured since the nineteenth century, with names such as Cadbury, Fry's, Rowntree and Lindt leading the way.

The complex process of converting cacao beans into chocolate requires the beans first to be cleaned and then roasted – during which their flavour is adjusted. Another process removes the shells from the roasted beans, or nibs. The nibs are then subjected to milling (or grinding), which also entails heating and which produces a thick liquid consisting of cocoa solids suspended in fat, or cocoa butter. Some of this is pressed to remove the cocoa butter – the remaining solids being converted into cocoa powder; the rest, intended for eating, is left to cool and harden off, producing a raw, unsweetened dark chocolate, which is then mixed with other ingredients such as sugar and flavourings such as vanilla (and, for milk chocolate, milk) to achieve the desired style of chocolate. The chocolate is then refined, by means of rollers, and combined with additional cocoa butter. In the next process, called conching, the refined chocolate is kneaded, over several hours or even days, to ensure flavour maturation (see page 30).

Finally the chocolate goes through a stabilisation process known as tempering before being poured into moulds and left to cool.

## Choosing the right chocolate

The variety of chocolate is almost endless, and choosing the perfect chocolate for your baking and ice cream making is no mean feat, with more than 500 different artisan brands in the UK alone.

When making ice cream containing chocolate I always make sure to use chocolate with at least 70 per cent cocoa solids (Green & Black's and Valrhona being my preferred brands), so that my chocolate is strong, dark and bittersweet. When this is combined with the milk and cream of the ice cream base, the colour is toned down a few shades to a caramel-brown and the flavour is slightly softened and more finely balanced between bitter and sweet.

## Tempering chocolate

Although chocolate is tempered during the manufacturing process, if you then simply heat it and cool it to add to your ice cream, without controlling the temperature correctly, this will result in a crystallisation of the cocoa butter content, producing crystals of different sizes and thus a very grainy and unpleasant texture. So some additional tempering is required.

To temper your chocolate, first chop it up evenly then put about two-thirds of it into a heatproof bowl. Run a little water into a saucepan and heat it gently. Place the mixing bowl on top, ensuring that the bottom of the bowl is not touching the water (otherwise the chocolate may burn). Alternatively, you can use a bain-marie, or double boiler.

Allow the chocolate to melt slowly, at no more than 50°C, measured on a sugar thermometer, while stirring constantly. Once it becomes liquid, turn off the heat, remove the bowl from the pan and set aside to cool. Add the remaining chocolate, place the sugar thermometer into the bowl of chocolate and continue to stir until it has cooled to a temperature around 35°C. Once this temperature has been reached, leave the chocolate to finish cooling or place it in the refrigerator until needed.

## A rich chocolate sauce

To make the ultimate, rich chocolate sauce, put 1 tablespoon of cold water, 50g of softened butter, 150g of caster sugar and 1 teaspoon of vanilla extract into a saucepan and gently heat. Melt and temper 100g of dark chocolate as described above. Set this aside to cool, then add it to the melted butter mixture. Whisk all of the ingredients to combine fully and return them to a gentle heat for about 5 minutes. Best served warm, drizzled over ice cream.

# *chocolate and rosemary ice cream*

**Rosemary is a perfect, if somewhat unusual, pairing with chocolate: it just works, adding great depth and an extra dimension. In this ice cream, it helps to create an earthy, aromatic flavour reminiscent of raw cocoa.**

200ml whole milk
1 sprig of rosemary
200g dark chocolate (at least 75 per cent cocoa solids)
300ml double cream
75g caster sugar
4 free-range egg yolks
100g dark muscovado sugar

Place the milk and rosemary in a mixing bowl, cover with cling film and leave in the fridge overnight to allow the flavour to infuse.

On the following day, temper the chocolate as described on page 111.

Strain the milk mixture through a sieve (discard the rosemary) and into a saucepan. Add the cream, the caster sugar and the chocolate and place over a low heat. Cook gently, stirring frequently, until the chocolate has melted; do not allow the mixture to boil or burn.

Place the egg yolks and muscovado sugar in a mixing bowl and whisk together, using a hand or electric mixer, until you have a thick and glossy paste.

Bring the milk and chocolate mixture back up to a simmer, then gradually pour it into the egg mixture, whisking all the time, until it is well incorporated.

Return the mixture to the saucepan and cook for about 10 minutes on a low-to-medium heat, stirring constantly, to prevent it from curdling, until it has thickened enough to coat the back of the spoon. Remove from heat.

Pour the mixture into a bowl or large jug and leave it to cool at room temperature. Then cover it with cling film and place it in the refrigerator to chill for at least 1 hour.

Following the manufacturer's instructions, pour the chilled mixture into your ice cream maker and set it to churn. Once it has finished churning, decant the partially frozen ice cream into a freezer-friendly container and leave it in the freezer to set solid.

If you do not have an ice cream maker, follow the instructions on page 25.

Remove the ice cream from the freezer about 15 minutes before serving so that it can soften slightly.

# double chocolate cookie ice cream

**Cookie dough ice cream, first popularised by Ben & Jerry's in the 1980s, has become one of the world's favourites in recent years, seeing huge annual sales at the checkouts. The heavy, sweet and indulgent ice cream presented here is my take on this ultimate comfort food.**

100g (approximately) soft, double chocolate chip cookies
100g dark chocolate (at least 70 per cent cocoa solids)
200ml whole milk
300ml double cream
150g caster sugar
6 egg yolks
$\frac{1}{2}$ teaspoon almond extract

Begin by roughly crushing the cookies and placing them in a bowl; set aside.

Temper the chocolate as described on page 111. Set aside to cool.

Pour the milk and cream into a saucepan along with 75g of the sugar. Place over a low-to-medium heat. Bring to a simmer, stirring frequently to ensure that the mixture doesn't burn; do not allow it to boil. Let it simmer for about 5 minutes, then remove from the heat and set aside, remembering to stir occasionally.

Place the egg yolks and remaining sugar in a mixing bowl and whisk together, using a hand or electric mixer, until you have a pale, thick and glossy paste.

Bring the milk mixture back up to a simmer, then gradually pour it into the egg mixture, whisking all the time, until it is well incorporated.

Return the mixture to the saucepan and place over a low heat. Fold in the melted chocolate and the almond extract. Continue cooking gently for about 10 minutes, stirring constantly, to prevent the mixture from curdling, until it has thickened enough to coat the back of the spoon. Remove from heat.

Pour the mixture into a bowl or large jug and leave it to cool at room temperature. Then cover it with cling film and place it in the refrigerator to chill for at least 1 hour.

Following the manufacturer's instructions, pour the chilled mixture into your ice cream maker and set it to churn. Once it has finished churning, decant the partially frozen ice cream into a freezer-friendly container and stir in the broken-up cookie pieces. Place the ice cream in the freezer to set solid.

If you do not have an ice cream maker, follow the instructions on page 25.

Remove the ice cream from the freezer about 15 minutes before serving so that it can soften slightly.

# *white chocolate ice cream*

Disgracefully unctuous, white chocolate is the bastard child to the real thing; containing no actual cocoa solids – merely cocoa butter, along with sugar, milk solids and salt – it's not even technically chocolate. White chocolate is however, wildly nostalgic, and this ice cream conjures up memories of happily munching on a Milky Bar as a child, while the addition of truffle oil (truly!) and a raspberry coulis makes this ice cream a superb, sophisticated dessert.

200ml double cream
200ml whole milk
1 tablespoon truffle oil
150g caster sugar
80g white chocolate, roughly chopped
4 large free-range egg yolks

Pour the cream, milk and oil into a medium or large, heavy-based saucepan, along with half the sugar and the white chocolate. Cook gently over a low heat, stirring at regular intervals, until the chocolate melts; do not let the mixture boil or burn. Remove from the heat and set aside, remembering to stir occasionally.

Place the egg yolks and remaining sugar in a mixing bowl and whisk together, using a hand or electric mixer, until you have a pale, thick and glossy paste.

Bring the milk and chocolate mixture back up to a simmer, then gradually pour it into the egg mixture, whisking all the time, until it is well incorporated.

Return the mixture to the saucepan and cook for about 10 minutes on a low-to-medium heat, stirring constantly, to prevent it from curdling, until it has thickened enough to coat the back of the spoon. Remove from heat.

Pour the mixture into a bowl or large jug and leave it to cool at room temperature. Then cover it with cling film and place it in the refrigerator to chill for at least 1 hour.

Following the manufacturer's instructions, pour the chilled mixture into your ice cream maker and set it to churn. Once it has finished churning, decant the partially frozen ice cream into a freezer-friendly container and leave it in the freezer to set solid.

If you do not have an ice cream maker, follow the instructions on page 25.

Remove the ice cream from the freezer about 15 minutes before serving so that it can soften slightly. Serve it with a raspberry coulis (see page 125).

# *simple choc ice*

**Consisting of soft-scoop vanilla ice cream encased in a hard crust of chocolate, the choc ice arrived in Britain in the 1960s, produced by Walls. It came in a paper wrapper and in two different flavours: the classic Chunky Choc Ice and its slight more exotic sister, Midnight Mint. Both became instant hits up and down the UK and remained popular into the 1990s. This recipe is my tribute to a very simple and delicious ice cream treat.**

### *makes 12 choc ices*

250ml double cream
200ml whole milk
120g vanilla sugar (see page 39)
1 teaspoon fresh lemon juice
1 teaspoon vanilla extract
5 free-range egg yolks
2 tablespoons skimmed milk powder

### *for the chocolate coating*

200g dark chocolate (at least 70 per cent
  cocoa solids)
50g milk chocolate
1 teaspoon vanilla extract

you will need a small ice cream scoop, about
  half the normal size

Begin by making the vanilla ice cream, following the recipe on page 47. Churn in your ice cream machine, but do not freeze; leave it in the machine for the moment.

Cover a large baking tray with kitchen foil. Using a small scoop, place groups of 3 small scoops of vanilla ice-cream in evenly spaced rows next to each other, making a total of 12 scoops. Place the tray in the freezer until the ice cream is hard.

Roughly chop the two chocolates into small pieces and place in a bain-marie, or mixing bowl set over simmering water; add the vanilla extract. Leave it to melt, stirring constantly. Once fully melted set it aside to cool.

Remove the ice cream scoops from the freezer and square each one up to form a rectangular shape, using a cake server or butter knife. Evenly spoon the dark chocolate over each block of ice cream; it should harden immediately. Tidy up with your knife and smooth the surface of each choc ice before returning to the freezer to set solid.

# dark chocolate and mandarin ice cream

This ice cream always reminds me of my childhood and a special treat Mum sometimes included in my packed lunch. Along with the sandwich, crisps and fruit, I'd find a chocolate and orange KitKat. Pure heaven – just like this ice cream, with its mellow chocolate contrasting with sharp citrus flavours. If you don't have any mandarins, two oranges will do the job just fine.

### for the mandarin syrup

2 large mandarins or oranges
1 heaped tablespoon caster sugar
2 tablespoons orange juice

200ml whole milk
250ml double cream
150g caster sugar
4 free-range egg yolks
100g dark chocolate, roughly chopped

segments of fresh mandarins or oranges,
    to serve

First make the mandarin/orange syrup. Divide each fruit into segments and roughly chop the segments into several pieces. Place them in a saucepan along with 2 tablespoons of cold water, a heaped tablespoon of caster sugar and the orange juice. Gently cook for 10–20 minutes, or until the ingredients have fully broken down and formed a thick syrup. Set aside to cool for use later.

Temper the chocolate as instructed on page 111 and set aside to cool.

For the ice cream, pour the milk and cream into a saucepan and add half the sugar; place over a low heat and cook gently, stirring at regular intervals, allowing the mixture to heat up, but not boil or burn. Remove from the heat and set aside, remembering to stir occasionally.

Place the egg yolks and the rest of the sugar in a mixing bowl and whisk together, using a hand or electric mixer, until you have a pale, thick and glossy paste.

Bring the milk mixture back up to a simmer, then gradually pour it into the egg mixture, whisking all the time, until it is well incorporated.

Return the mixture to the saucepan. Whisk together to ensure all the ingredients are well combined, then fold in the chocolate. Cook for about 10 minutes on a low-to-medium heat, stirring constantly, to prevent it from curdling, until it has thickened enough to coat the back of the spoon. Remove from heat.

Stir the strained mandarin syrup into the ice cream base. Then pour the mixture into a bowl or large jug and leave it to cool at room temperature. Cover it with cling film and place it in the refrigerator to chill for at least 1 hour.

Following the manufacturer's instructions, pour the chilled ice cream mixture into your ice cream maker and set it to churn. Once it has finished churning, decant the partially frozen ice cream into a freezer-friendly container and leave it in the freezer to set solid.

Remove the ice cream from the freezer at least 15 minutes before serving to allow it to soften enough to scoop. Serve it with segments of fresh mandarins or oranges.

# dark chocolate and wild cherry ice cream

Bursting with sour, bitter and sweet flavours, this ice cream packs a punch. When making it at home I like to enhance the flavour by adding some cherry liqueur; alternatively feel free to substitute your own favourite fruit liqueur or juice. The hot fudge sauce sets off the ice cream perfectly.

100g dark chocolate (at least 70 per cent cocoa solids), roughly chopped
250ml double cream
200ml whole milk
150g caster sugar
5 free-range egg yolks
10–15 wild or morello cherries, stoned and halved
2 teaspoons cherry liqueur (optional)

### for the hot fudge sauce
200g ($^1/_2$ tin) condensed milk
250g dark chocolate (at least 70 per cent cocoa solids), broken into small pieces

Temper the chocolate as instructed on page 111 and set aside to cool.

Pour the cream and milk into a saucepan; add half the caster sugar and the chocolate. Cook gently over a low heat, stirring frequently, until the chocolate has melted; take care not to let the mixture boil or burn. Let it simmer for about 5 minutes, then remove from the heat and set aside, remembering to stir occasionally.

Place the egg yolks and sugar in a mixing bowl and whisk together, using a hand or electric mixer, until you have a pale, thick and glossy paste.

Bring the milk and chocolate mixture back up to a simmer, then gradually pour it into the egg mixture, whisking all the time, until it is well incorporated.

Return the mixture to the saucepan and add the cherries and optional cherry liqueur. Cook for about 10 minutes on a low-to-medium heat, stirring constantly, to prevent it from curdling, until it has thickened enough to coat the back of the spoon. Remove from heat.

Pour the mixture into a bowl or large jug and leave it to cool at room temperature. Then cover it with cling film and place it in the refrigerator to chill for at least 1 hour.

Following the manufacturer's instructions, pour the chilled mixture into your ice cream maker and set it to churn. Once it has finished churning, decant the partially frozen ice cream into a freezer-friendly container and leave it in the freezer to set solid.

If you do not have an ice cream maker, follow the instructions on page 25.

Remove the ice cream from the freezer about 15 minutes before serving so that it can soften slightly.

To make the hot fudge sauce, place a bowl over a pan of just-simmering water, taking care to ensure the bowl is not touching the water. Add the condensed milk and chocolate pieces to the bowl and heat for 10–12 minutes, stirring occasionally until you have a lovely thick fudgy sauce. Serve immediately over the ice cream, and with a Tuile (see page 275) on the side.

# white chocolate raspberry ripple ice cream

**Ultra-sweet, white chocolate and raspberry ripple ice cream is delicious, unbelievably simple to make and visually stunning. The ripple effect is easy to achieve with a flat butter knife and can be used in all sorts of ice creams, as your fancy takes you. For a soft texture this recipe uses pectin or gelatine in place of egg.**

200g white chocolate, broken roughly into
    small pieces
300ml whole milk
1 sheet of pectin/gelatine (20–25g)
300ml double cream
$^1/_2$ tablespoon cornflour

### for the raspberry coulis
150g raspberries
2 teaspoons lemon juice
2 tablespoons icing sugar

First melt the white chocolate. Place it in a bain-marie (double boiler) over simmering water; stir it as it melts to stop it from burning. Once melted, set it aside to cool.

Place the milk in a saucepan over a medium heat, along with the pectin or gelatine, and slowly bring to a simmer, stirring constantly until the pectin/gelatine has completely melted. Then pour in the cream and continue to heat for a further 5 minutes.

When the mixture has thickened enough to coat the back of a spoon, add the cornflour and fold in the melted white chocolate. Continue to cook and stir until all of the ingredients have fully dissolved and combined.

Pour the mixture into a bowl or large jug and leave it to cool at room temperature. Then cover it with cling film and place it in the refrigerator to chill for at least 1 hour.

Meanwhile make the raspberry coulis. Heat the raspberries, lemon juice and caster sugar in a saucepan until the sugar has fully dissolved and the raspberries begin to break down. As the fruit softens, add a teaspoon of cold water, stir, and continue to heat for a further 10 minutes. Then remove from the heat and set aside to cool. Blend in a food processor or blender until smooth and pass through a fine sieve to remove the seeds; set aside for use later.

Following the manufacturer's instructions, pour the chilled ice cream mixture into your ice cream maker and set it to churn. Once it has finished churning, decant the partially frozen ice cream into a freezer-friendly container and pour a few tablespoons of the raspberry coulis on top. Using a knife, swirl it through the ice cream. Place the ice cream in the freezer to set solid.

If you do not have an ice cream maker, follow the instructions on page 25. Add the raspberry coulis and swirl it through the ice cream after the container has been in the freezer for 1 hour.

Remove the ice cream from the freezer about 15 minutes before serving so that it can soften slightly.

# *double chocolate knickerbocker glory*

This decadent version of the knickerbocker glory (see the more traditional fruit-based one on page 161) is smooth, dark and chocolatey – what more could you want from a dessert? Enjoy making your way through the layers of vanilla and chocolate ice cream topped with lashings of whipped cream and chocolate sauce.

### makes 2 servings

### for the chocolate sauce
100g dark chocolate (at least 70 per cent cocoa solids), roughly chopped
25g caster sugar
50g unsalted butter

### for the Bourbon vanilla ice cream
200ml whole milk
350ml double cream
120g caster sugar
1 vanilla pod, split lengthways
1 tablespoon Madagascan vanilla extract
5 large free-range egg yolks

### for the chocolate ice cream
200g dark chocolate (at least 75 per cent cocoa solids)
200ml whole milk
300ml double cream
4 free-range egg yolks
75g caster sugar
100g dark muscovado sugar
4 free-range egg yolks

### to assemble
150ml double or whipping cream
1 teaspoon caster sugar
50g dark chocolate (at least 75 per cent cocoa solids), roughly chopped into small pieces
about 15g chopped walnuts or pecans (optional)

First make the chocolate sauce. Melt the chocolate, sugar and butter in a bain-marie (double boiler) over simmering water, making sure that the bowl or upper pan does not touch the surface of the water; otherwise the chocolate is likely to burn. Once the ingredients have melted and are fully combined, set the sauce aside to cool for use later.

Using the recipe on page 48 make a fresh batch of Bourbon vanilla ice cream.

Now make a batch of chocolate ice cream. First temper the chocolate as instructed on page 111. Set aside to cool.

Next, pour the milk and cream into a saucepan and place over a low-to-medium heat. Bring to a simmer, stirring frequently to ensure that the mixture doesn't burn; do not allow it to boil. Let it simmer for about 5 minutes, then remove from the heat and set aside, remembering to stir occasionally.

Place the egg yolks, caster sugar and muscovado sugar in a mixing bowl and whisk together, using a hand or electric mixer, until you have a pale, thick and glossy paste.

Bring the milk mixture back up to a simmer, then gradually pour it into the egg mixture, whisking all the time, until it is well incorporated.

Return the mixture to the saucepan and cook for about 10 minutes on a low-to-medium heat, stirring constantly, to prevent it from curdling, until it has thickened enough to coat the back of the spoon. Remove from heat and leave to cool slightly.

Fold in the tempered chocolate. Pour the mixture into a bowl or large jug and leave it to cool at room temperature. Then cover it with cling film and place it in the refrigerator to chill for at least 1 hour.

Following the manufacturer's instructions, pour the chilled mixture into your ice cream maker and set it to churn. Once it has finished

churning, decant the partially frozen ice cream into a freezer-friendly container and leave it in the freezer to set solid.

If you do not have an ice cream maker, follow the instructions on page 25.

Remove both ice creams from the freezer about 15 minutes before serving so that they can soften slightly.

Add the sugar to the double/whipping cream and whip the cream until it forms soft peaks.

Now assemble the knickerbocker glory. Line each sundae glass with the chocolate sauce, turning the glass so that the inside is coated with sauce. Fill the bottom of the glass with some chocolate chips, followed by a generous helping of chocolate sauce and alternate layers of vanilla and chocolate ice cream, topped off with more chocolate sauce, whipped cream, the remaining chocolate chips and the optional chopped nuts.

# *dark chocolate sorbet*

**The perfect recipe for an absolute beginner, this sorbet couldn't be simpler to make. All it needs is a quick and easy sugar syrup base, melted chocolate and a little patience. Your ice cream maker or freezer (if you don't have an ice cream machine) will do most of the work. Dark chocolate has a bitter, clean taste, perfect for cleansing and refreshing the palate after a rich meal.**

200g dark chocolate (at least 70 per cent
   cocoa solids), roughly chopped
350ml tepid water
1 teaspoon lemon juice
100g caster sugar

Temper the chocolate as instructed on page 111.

Pour the water, lemon juice and caster sugar into a saucepan and bring to a gentle simmer, stirring until all of the sugar has dissolved and the mixture thickens to a syrupy consistency.

Whisk the melted chocolate into the sugar syrup until all the ingredients are fully combined. Then increase the heat and continue to whisk for a few more minutes. Then take it off the heat, pour into a bowl or large jug and set aside to cool.

Once cool, cover it with cling film and place it in the refrigerator to chill for 1 hour.

Following the manufacturer's instructions, pour the chilled sorbet mixture into your ice cream maker and set it to churn. Once it has finished churning, decant the partially frozen sorbet into a freezer-friendly container and leave it in the freezer to set solid.

If you do not have an ice cream maker, follow the instructions on page 25.

Remove the sorbet from the freezer about 15 minutes before serving so that it can soften slightly.

# choc 'n' nut ice lolly

The basic choc ice lends itself to various refinements and embellishments – as the producers of the ever-popular Magnum have proved. You can create your own glorified choc ice at home using Bourbon Vanilla Ice Cream, chocolate sauce and some chopped nuts for a crunchy texture.

*makes 10–12 choc ices*

### for the Bourbon vanilla ice cream

1 vanilla pod
500ml double cream
400ml whole milk
180g caster sugar
6 large free-range egg yolks
1 tablespoon Madagascan vanilla extract

### for the chocolate coating

100g whole blanched hazelnuts
200g of dark chocolate, at least 70% cocoa
   solids
20g of cocoa powder

Following the recipe on page 48, make a batch of Bourbon Vanilla ice cream. After chilling the mixture as instructed, place it in your ice cream maker for 1 hour to freeze and churn.

Meanwhile, line a baking tray with baking parchment and fit a piping bag with a 2cm nozzle. Spoon the partially frozen ice cream into the bag and pipe the soft ice cream in long lengths on to the lined baking tray. Place in the freezer for 5–6 hours to freeze hard.

Now make the chocolate and nut coating. Heat the oven to 150°C/Gas Mark 2 and line another baking tray with kitchen foil. Toast the nuts until golden, which should take 8–10 minutes. Blitz in a blender until chopped into small pieces. Place the nuts in a coarse sieve and shake gently to get rid of all the excess powder, as this would thicken the chocolate. Weigh the remaining nuts to make sure you have at least 50g and leave to cool. (Any excess can be saved for topping other ice creams.)

Melt the chocolate and cocoa powder in a mixing bowl over a pan of simmering water or in a bain-marie (double boiler), stirring almost constantly to combine and avoid burning. Mix in the hazelnuts and keep warm.

Cut the frozen lengths of ice cream into 8cm-long pieces, and push a lolly stick into each. Return to the freezer to keep frozen. Line another baking tray with baking parchment, in readiness for the finished choc ices.

Once they are solid again, dip each ice cream length into the mixing bowl of melted chocolate and hazelnuts. On contact with the ice cream, the coating will quickly set firm. Immediately place the choc ice on the lined tray and move on to the next. Place the tray of covered choc ices in the freezer for a further hour before serving.

# bombes

A bombe is a rounded shape of two or more layers of ice cream which is then often covered with chocolate. Once the chocolate has been poured over the ice cream, the bombe can be quickly rolled in cocoa, cinnamon and/or toasted nuts. There is plenty of scope here to get very creative.

### makes 8 bombes

### for the Bourbon vanilla ice cream
500ml double cream
400ml whole milk
1 vanilla pod
180g caster sugar
6 large free-range egg yolks
1 tablespoon Madagascan vanilla extract

### for the chocolate ice cream
200g dark chocolate (at least 75 per cent
  cocoa solids)
200ml whole milk
300ml double cream
4 free-range egg yolks
100g dark muscovado sugar
75g caster sugar
4 free-range egg yolks

### for the coating
100g dark chocolate (at least 70 per cent
  cocoa solids)
25g cocoa powder
25g ground cinnamon
25g toasted flaked almonds

Make a fresh batch of both the Bourbon Vanilla and the Chocolate ice cream, following the recipes on pages 48 and 161 respectively. Line 2 dinner plates with baking parchment and place in the freezer for 1 hour to cool the surface temperature.

Temper the chocolate as instructed on page 111; set aside to cool a little.

Remove the plates from the freezer. Also remove the two ice creams and allow them to soften a little for 15 minutes. Place an ice cream scoop, a flat knife and 4 dessertspoons nearby in your working area and have ready a baking tray, which will be a useful surface when covering the ice cream with chocolate – a potentially messy procedure. Also have within easy reach the melted chocolate, a dish containing the cocoa powder and cinnamon, mixed together, and another dish containing the flaked almonds.

Using a small scoop, place 8 half balls of vanilla ice cream on to one of the plates in rows, leaving a few centimetres' gap between balls. Clean the scoop off and scoop a further 8 half balls of chocolate ice cream on top of the vanilla half balls, pressing firmly down on each. Using your fingers or a flat knife, round each ball off neatly to form a sphere.

Working as quickly as possible and holding the ice cream balls in place on the baking tray, use a dessertspoon to pour the melted chocolate over each ball, encasing it completely; use another dessertspoon to manipulate it. Dust each ball with cocoa powder and ground cinnamon and place it on the remaining dinner plate. Sprinkle toasted almonds over each bombe and gently push them into the coating.

Place the plate of bombes into the freezer to set solid. When solid, remove from the freezer, peel each bombe from the baking parchment and serve.

berries

*berri*

From the sweet, vivid strawberry and the soft little pink raspberry to the overpoweringly sour blackberry with its dark purple, rich, blue hue – Britain's hedgerows and supermarket shelves offer a profusion of berries each spring, summer and autumn. What we don't grow, we import, which gives us exotic and out-of-season fruit any time of the year.

This chapter features some of my favourite recipes, including the likes of Blackberries & Cream and Strawberry Pavlova ice cream and my own versions of classic desserts such as Eton Mess, gooseberry fool and frozen yoghurt.

### *When to pick wild berries*

When foraging for your own berries – as opposed to using shop- bought ones – it is very important to understand exactly when different varieties of berry are in season. From May until August gooseberries are abundant, while from July through September and sometimes right up until October both blackberries and wild strawberries come into season (both of these, by the way, are extremely rich in vitamin C). Raspberries can be found from May into July, whereas wild cherries, rich in both flavour and colour, have a much shorter season: from mid-June until the end of July. Finally, sloes are usually available from the start of August right up until the very beginning of December, depending upon when the first frost falls.

*es*

### The ultimate fruit coulis

This richly flavoured fruit coulis, using a
variety of berries is perfect for lavishly
pouring over your ice creams or sorbets.
Thoroughly wash 50g of raspberries,
blackberries, strawberries (wild, if available),
gooseberries and cranberries (these can be
frozen when they are available, around
Christmastime, and kept until needed).
Tip them into a saucepan, cover with
125g caster sugar and add 5 tablespoons
of cold water. Cover the pan and heat for
10 minutes on a low heat. Remove the lid and
vigorously stir the fruit; by now the berries
should be breaking down, the sugar should
have dissolved and the mixture should have
begun to thicken. Continue to heat without
the lid for a further 10 minutes. Set the
saucepan aside to cool, then pour the fruit
into a blender or food processor and blitz on
full speed for about 3–5 minutes until no big
lumps of fruit remain. Pass the purée through
a fine sieve to remove the seeds. Decant the
puréed mixture into a bowl or jug, cover and
set in the fridge to chill until needed.

# blackberries and cream ice cream

With its deep purple hue, thanks to a sharp blackberry coulis, this ice cream looks beautiful as well as tasting fantastic. The recipe is based on the flavour we sell at Winstone's Ice Cream, which in 2012 became one of our best-sellers. When you make it, you will see why.

300g blackberries
3 tablespoons fresh lemon juice
150g caster sugar
200ml whole milk
250ml double cream
5 free-range egg yolks

In a blender or food processor, mix together the blackberries, lemon juice, half the sugar and the milk, until the mixture is a smooth liquid. Pass through a fine sieve to remove the seeds.

In a medium saucepan, heat the cream to the simmering point over a low-to-medium heat; continue simmering for about 5 minutes, stirring frequently to ensure that the mixture doesn't burn; do not allow it to boil. Remove it from the heat and set aside, remembering to stir occasionally.

Place the egg yolks and remaining sugar in a mixing bowl and whisk together, using a hand or electric mixer, until you have a pale, thick and glossy paste.

Bring the cream back up to a simmer, then gradually pour it into the egg mixture, whisking all the time, until it is well incorporated.

Return the mixture to the saucepan and cook for about 10 minutes on a low-to-medium heat, stirring constantly, to prevent it from curdling, until it has thickened enough to coat the back of the spoon. Remove from heat.

Stir in the blackberry and milk mixture and cook gently for 5 minutes. Remove from heat. (If you prefer a 'ripple' effect to the ice cream, you can remove from the heat and gently fold the blackberry and milk mixture very loosely into the base mix instead.)

Pour the mixture into a bowl or large jug and leave it to cool at room temperature. Then cover it with cling film and place it in the refrigerator to chill for at least 1 hour.

Following the manufacturer's instructions, pour the chilled mixture into your ice cream maker and set it to churn. Once it has finished churning, decant the partially frozen ice cream into a freezer-friendly container and leave it in the freezer to set solid.

If you do not have an ice cream maker, follow the instructions on page 25.

Remove the ice cream from the freezer about 15 minutes before serving so that it can soften slightly.

# *blueberry pie ice cream*

Thought to have first been enjoyed by American settlers, thanks to the abundance of wild blueberries in states such as Maine, the blueberry pie remains a firm favourite, with its traditional butter crust and soft, sweet, fruit filling. In my attempt to emulate the mighty blueberry pie, I have used mascarpone instead of cream to produce a milder-tasting ice cream base with a much lighter texture.

150g blueberries
1 teaspoon brown sugar
a dash of lemon juice
50g caster sugar
2 teaspoons cornflour
4 free-range egg yolks
1 teaspoon vanilla extract
250ml whole milk
200g mascarpone
50g digestive biscuits, crushed

Begin by puréeing the blueberries. Place them in a blender or food processor, along with the brown sugar, the lemon juice and a teaspoon of cold water, and blend until all of the ingredients are fully combined. Set aside for later.

In a mixing bowl, whisk together the caster sugar, cornflour, egg yolks and vanilla extract until they form a thick, pale, paste-like substance.

Place the milk, puréed blueberries and mascarpone in a saucepan and cook over a low heat for 5 minutes, stirring; do not allow to boil.

Remove from the heat and fold in the egg mixture. Now, using a hand or electric mixer, whisk until all of the ingredients are fully combined. Return to a gentle heat for a further 5 minutes or until the mixture is thick enough to coat the back of a spoon.

Pour the mixture into a bowl or large jug and leave it to cool at room temperature. Then cover it with cling film and place it in the refrigerator to chill for 1 hour.

Following the manufacturer's instructions, pour the chilled ice cream mixture into your ice cream maker and set it to churn. Once it has finished churning, stir the crushed digestive biscuits into the partially frozen ice cream. Decant the ice cream into a freezer-friendly container and leave it in the freezer to set solid.

If you do not have an ice cream maker, follow the instructions on page 25.

Remove the ice cream from the freezer about 15 minutes before serving so that it can soften slightly.

# eton mess ice cream

**Named for Eton College, the luscious dessert Eton Mess has, according to tradition, been served at the school's annual cricket match with rival Winchester College for more than 100 years, and it has become a great favourite at summer parties all over the country. Consisting of a melange of juicy strawberries, cream and crushed meringue, it lends itself perfectly to being reinterpreted as ice cream.**

150ml whole milk
150ml double cream
1 large free-range egg yolk
150g caster sugar
50g raspberries, washed and hulled
250g strawberries, washed and hulled
1 teaspoon vanilla extract
a dash of lemon juice
50g broken meringues

Begin by making meringues, following the recipe on page 271 (but simply spooning the mixture on to the baking tray, rather than forming nests). When baked and cooled, measure out about 50g of meringues, crush them into small pieces and set aside for later.

Pour the milk and cream into a saucepan and place over a low-to-medium heat. Bring to a simmer, stirring frequently to ensure that the mixture doesn't burn; do not allow it to boil. Let it simmer for about 5 minutes, then remove from the heat and set aside, remembering to stir occasionally.

Place the egg yolk and sugar in a mixing bowl and whisk together, using a hand or electric mixer, until you have a pale, thick and glossy paste.

Bring the milk mixture back up to a simmer, then gradually pour it into the egg mixture, whisking all the time, until it is well incorporated.

Return the mixture to the saucepan and cook for about 10 minutes on a low-to-medium heat, stirring constantly, to prevent it from curdling, until it has thickened enough to coat the back of the spoon. Remove from heat.

Place the raspberries and 150g of the strawberries in a blender or food processor, along with the vanilla extract, the lemon juice and 2 tablespoons of water. Blend to a smooth purée, adding a little more water if it seems too thick. Stir the puréed fruit mixture into the custard and gently heat for a further 10 minutes to allow the flavours to infuse, giving the custard constant attention to avoid burning. Remove from the heat.

Pour the mixture into a bowl or large jug and leave it to cool at room temperature. Then cover it with cling film and place it in the refrigerator to chill for at least 1 hour.

Following the manufacturer's instructions, pour the chilled ice cream mixture into your ice cream maker and set it to churn. Once it has finished churning, decant the partially frozen ice cream into a freezer-friendly container. Roughly chop the remaining strawberries and mix them into the ice cream, along with the broken meringues. Place the ice cream in the freezer to set solid.

If you do not have an ice cream maker, follow the instructions on page 25, folding in the chopped strawberries and broken meringues just before placing the ice cream in the freezer for the first time.

Remove the ice cream from the freezer about 15 minutes before serving so that it can soften slightly.

# *summer fruit parfait*

**Meaning 'perfect' in French, a parfait is
very simple to make because you don't
need to churn it. The parfait sets only
partially solid. Summer fruits – any
seasonal berries you fancy – and crushed
meringue make this parfait similar in
flavour to Eton Mess ice cream (page
142), but different in look and texture.**

100ml whole milk
4 large free-range egg yolks
200g vanilla sugar (see page 39)
250g fresh summer berries, washed and
    hulled
a dash of fresh lemon juice
250ml double cream
1 tablespoon vanilla extract
50g broken meringues

### *To decorate*
150g fresh berries
75g clotted cream

Begin by making the meringues, following the
recipe on page 271 (but simply spooning the
mixture on to the baking tray, rather than
forming nests). When baked and cooled,
measure out about 50g of meringues, crush
them into small pieces and set aside for later.

In a saucepan mix together the milk, the
egg yolks and half the vanilla sugar; place
over a low heat and bring to a simmer.
Continue to cook gently for 10 minutes,
stirring constantly and ensuring that the
mixture does not boil. Once the mixture
begins to thicken, set aside to cool.

Blitz the berries in a blender or food
processor; add the lemon juice and continue
to blend until the mixture is completely
smooth.

Pour the cream into a mixing bowl and
whisk until it forms smooth, velvety, stiff
peaks. Gently fold in the puréed fruit, the
milk and egg yolk mixture, the vanilla extract
and the broken-up meringues.

Line a standard 900g loaf tin with baking
parchment. Pour the mixture into the loaf tin
and place in the freezer to set solid.

To serve, remove from the freezer, decorate
with fresh fruit and serve by the slice with a
generous helping of clotted cream.

# gooseberry fool ice cream

The creamy English dessert called a 'fool' (the origin of the name is obscure) is thought to date back to the fifteenth century and to have originally been made with gooseberries. Since then, it has often been made with other fruits. In this ice cream, a touch of freshly squeezed lemon juice enhances the subtle flavour of the gooseberries.

300g gooseberries
a dash of lemon juice
200ml whole milk
200ml double cream
5 free-range egg yolks
150g caster sugar

Place the gooseberries in a blender or food processor along with the lemon juice and blitz until you have a smooth purée.

Pour the milk and cream into a saucepan and place over a low-to-medium heat. Bring to a simmer, stirring frequently to ensure that the mixture doesn't burn; do not allow it to boil. Let it simmer for about 5 minutes, then remove from the heat and set aside, remembering to stir occasionally.

Place the egg yolks and sugar in a mixing bowl and whisk together, using a hand or electric mixer, until you have a pale, thick and glossy paste.

Bring the milk mixture back up to a simmer, then gradually pour it into the egg mixture, whisking all the time, until it is well incorporated.

Return the mixture to the saucepan and cook for about 10 minutes on a low-to-medium heat, stirring constantly, to prevent it from curdling, until it has thickened enough to coat the back of the spoon. Remove from heat.

Stir in the gooseberry purée. Pour the mixture into a bowl or large jug and leave it to cool at room temperature. Then cover it with cling film and place it in the refrigerator to chill for at least 1 hour.

Following the manufacturer's instructions, pour the chilled mixture into your ice cream maker and set it to churn. Once it has finished churning, decant the partially frozen ice cream into a freezer-friendly container and leave it in the freezer to set solid.

If you do not have an ice cream maker, follow the instructions on page 25.

Remove the ice cream from the freezer about 15 minutes before serving so that it can soften slightly.

# strawberries and cream ice cream

There are good reasons why strawberry is one of the three most popular flavours of ice cream on the planet (alongside vanilla and chocolate, of course).
At their best, strawberries are sweet, juicy, vivid in colour and rich in flavour. With the addition of lemon juice to enhance the flavour, clotted cream and a sprinkle of black pepper, this recipe will leave you wanting more.

300g strawberries, washed and hulled
1 teaspoon lemon juice
100ml whole milk
200ml double cream
6 large free-range egg yolks
150g caster sugar
1 tablespoon clotted cream
1 teaspoon freshly ground black pepper

Put the strawberries, along with the lemon juice and a teaspoon of water in a blender or food processor and blitz until they are completely liquid and free of lumps. Pass the fruit through a fine sieve to remove any unwanted seeds and set aside.

Pour the milk and cream into a saucepan and place over a low-to-medium heat. Bring to a simmer, stirring frequently to ensure that the mixture doesn't burn; do not allow it to boil. Let it simmer for about 5 minutes, then remove from the heat and set aside, remembering to stir occasionally.

Place the egg yolks and sugar in a mixing bowl and whisk together, using a hand or electric mixer, until you have a pale, thick and glossy paste.

Bring the milk mixture back up to a simmer, then gradually pour it into the egg mixture, whisking all the time, until it is well incorporated.

Return the mixture to the saucepan and cook for about 10 minutes on a low-to-medium heat, stirring constantly, to prevent it from curdling, until it has thickened enough to coat the back of the spoon. Remove from heat.

Stir in the strawberry purée and the clotted cream and scrape the bottom of the pan to ensure that the mixture has combined, then whisk with an electric mixer for 5 minutes.

Pour the mixture into a bowl or large jug and leave it to cool at room temperature. Then cover it with cling film and place it in the refrigerator to chill for at least 1 hour.

Following the manufacturer's instructions, pour the chilled ice cream mixture into your ice cream maker and set it to churn. Once it has finished churning, decant the partially frozen ice cream into a freezer-friendly container, mix in the black pepper and leave it in the freezer to set solid.

If you do not have an ice cream maker, follow the instructions on page 25.

Remove the ice cream from the freezer about 15 minutes before serving so that it can soften slightly.

# *strawberry pavlova ice cream*

Created in the 1920s in honour of the Russian ballerina Anna Pavlova, the dessert known as a pavlova consists of soft, chewy meringue, fresh fruit and lashings of whipped cream – ingredients that also make for a perfect ice cream, full of flavour and texture.

300g strawberries, washed and hulled
a dash of lemon juice
150ml whole milk
250ml double cream
5 large organic free-range egg yolks
150g vanilla sugar (see page 39)
75g meringues, roughly crushed

Following the recipe on page 271 bake a fresh batch of meringues (do not bother to form nests), crush 3 or 4, to make up required weight, and set aside until ready.

Place the strawberries in a blender or food processor, along with the lemon juice, and blitz until liquid.

Pour the milk and cream into a saucepan and place over a low-to-medium heat. Bring to a simmer, stirring frequently to ensure that the mixture doesn't burn; do not allow it to boil. Let it simmer for about 5 minutes, then remove from the heat and set aside, remembering to stir occasionally.

Place the egg yolks and sugar in a mixing bowl and whisk together, using a hand or electric mixer, until you have a pale, thick and glossy paste.

Bring the milk mixture back up to a simmer, then gradually pour it into the egg mixture, whisking all the time, until it is well incorporated.

Return the mixture to the saucepan and cook for about 10 minutes on a low-to-medium heat, stirring constantly, to prevent it from curdling, until it has thickened enough to coat the back of the spoon. Remove from heat. Stir in the strawberry purée, scraping the bottom of the pan to ensure the ingredients have combined thoroughly.

Pour the mixture into a bowl or large jug and leave it to cool at room temperature. Then place it in the refrigerator to chill for at least 1 hour.

Following the manufacturer's instructions, pour the chilled ice cream mixture into your ice cream maker and set it to churn. Once it has finished churning, decant the partially frozen ice cream into a freezer-friendly container, then whisk it, using a hand whisk, for 5 minutes to allow further incorporation of air and so ensure a soft, smooth texture. Stir in the meringue pieces, then leave the ice cream in the freezer to set solid.

If you do not have an ice cream maker, follow the instructions on page 25, adding the meringue pieces just before placing the ice cream in the freezer for the first time.

Remove the ice cream from the freezer about 15 minutes before serving so that it can soften slightly.

# *balsamic, blackberry and strawberry ice cream*

**The va-va-voom version of strawberry ice cream. Sure, plain strawberry ice cream is delicious, but why settle for simplicity when you can have magnificence?**

225ml whole milk
150ml double cream
160g caster sugar
3 tablespoons lemon juice
3 free-range egg yolks
200g strawberries, washed and hulled
125g blackberries, washed
100ml balsamic vinegar

Pour the milk and cream into a medium saucepan and place over a low-to-medium heat. Bring to a simmer; add half the sugar and the lemon juice and cook over a low heat, stirring at regular intervals, for 10 minutes. Do not allow the mixture to boil. Remove from the heat.

Whisk the egg yolks and the remaining sugar in a mixing bowl, with a hand or electric mixer, for about 2 minutes, or until the mixture has thickened to a smooth, pale paste.

Put the strawberries, blackberries and balsamic vinegar into a blender or food processor and blend until smooth. Strain the mixture through a fine sieve into a bowl.

Bring the milk mixture back up to a simmer, then gradually pour it into the egg mixture, whisking all the time until it is well combined.

Return the mixture to the saucepan and cook for about 10 minutes on a low-to-medium heat, stirring constantly, to prevent it from curdling, until it has thickened enough to coat the back of the spoon. Remove from heat.

Add the berry mixture and stir well to incorporate. (If you prefer a 'ripple' effect to the ice cream, you can remove from the heat and gently fold the berry mixture very loosely into the base mix instead.)

Pour the mixture into a bowl or large jug and leave it to cool at room temperature. Then place it in the refrigerator to chill for at least 1 hour.

Following the manufacturer's instructions, pour the chilled ice cream mixture into your ice cream maker and set it to churn. Once it has finished churning, decant the partially frozen ice cream into a freezer-friendly container and leave it in the freezer to set solid.

If you do not have an ice cream maker, follow the instructions on page 25.

Remove the ice cream from the freezer about 15 minutes before serving so that it can soften slightly.

# pink champagne and raspberry sorbet

Aside from being tasty and growing all over the countryside, raspberries are super fruits and have loads of nutritional benefits: they're packed with antioxidants (50 per cent more than strawberries) and are rich in fibre. They make fabulous ice cream and sorbet. The sugar syrup base of this sorbet balances the tartness of the raspberries, which in turn helps to bring out the complex flavour notes in the Champagne – as well as turning it pink!

100g caster sugar, plus a little extra to taste
250ml Champagne (or other dry sparkling wine)
500g fresh raspberries, washed
juice of 1 lemon
2 tablespoons cold water

Pour the 100g of caster sugar and the Champagne into a saucepan and place over a medium heat. Heat the pan gently, stirring, until the sugar has completely dissolved. Now bring to a simmer; you should see bubbles rising to the surface. Continue to cook these ingredients for at least 5 minutes, without stirring, during which time the liquid should begin to thicken to the consistency of a syrup.

Put the raspberries in another pan. Add the lemon juice, cover with a few teaspoons of caster sugar and the cold water, and simmer over a low heat for a couple of minutes until the fruit begins to soften and break down. Remove from the heat and leave to cool.

Once cool, pour the mixture into a blender or food processor and blitz until the fruit is a smooth purée.

Push the puréed fruit mixture through a fine sieve into a bowl, to remove all the seeds. Using a hand or electric whisk, combine it with the Champagne syrup.

Pour the mixture into a bowl or large jug, cover it with cling film and place it in the refrigerator to chill for at least 1 hour.

Following the manufacturer's instructions, pour the chilled sorbet mixture into your ice cream maker and set it to churn. Once it has finished churning, decant the partially frozen sorbet into a freezer-friendly container and leave it in the freezer to set solid.

If you do not have an ice cream maker, follow the instructions on page 25.

Remove the sorbet from the freezer about 15 minutes before serving so that it can soften slightly.

# *wild berries frozen yoghurt*

Popularised in the 1970s, frozen yoghurt is relatively low in fat and calories, light in texture and big in flavour. It's particularly delicious with fresh fruit and really very simple to make at home. This recipe uses Greek yoghurt and plenty of fresh berries, and tastes even better when topped with a spoonful of maple syrup and plenty of toasted pecans.

250g raspberries, washed
150g strawberries, washed and hulled
100g blackberries, washed
250g Greek yoghurt
125g caster sugar
1 teaspoon lemon juice

Roughly chop half the raspberries, strawberries and blackberries and set them aside. Place the rest in a food processor or blender and blitz to a fine purée; push this through a fine sieve to remove any seeds, which would make the frozen yoghurt bitter.

Place the purée in a saucepan, along with the Greek yoghurt; stir to combine, then gently stir in the caster sugar and lemon juice. Mix well, then gently heat for 5 minutes over a low heat to dissolve the sugar.

Remove from the heat. Pour the mixture into a bowl or large jug and leave it to cool at room temperature. Fold in the chopped berries. Then cover with cling film and place it in the refrigerator to chill for at least 1 hour.

Following the manufacturer's instructions, pour the chilled mixture into your ice cream maker and set it to churn. Once it has finished churning, decant the partially frozen yoghurt into a freezer-friendly container and leave it in the freezer to set solid.

If you do not have an ice cream maker, pour the chilled yoghurt into a loaf tin lined with baking parchment. Place it in the freezer for 2 hours, then remove and vigorously whisk with a fork to stop any large ice crystals from forming. Repeat after another 2 hours, then leave to set solid.

Remove the frozen yoghurt from the freezer about 15 minutes before serving so that it can soften slightly.

# raspberry kulfi

**Popular in India and the Middle East, kulfi is made from evaporated sweetened condensed milk. It has a thick, smooth texture and subtle caramel flavour, which here marries beautifully with tart raspberries to make a delicious alternative to ice cream.**

*this recipe will make 3 servings*

large handful of frozen raspberries, plus extra
   for decoration
1 tin (397g) sweetened condensed milk
3 tablespoons caster sugar
2 tablespoons vanilla extract

Place the raspberries (reserving a few for decoration) and the remaining ingredients in a blender or food processor and blend for 1 minute at a medium speed. This should produce a thick, mousse-like texture. If the mixture is too liquid, add a little more sugar; if it's too thick, continue to blend for another 30 seconds or so.

Once fully mixed, transfer the mixture to a saucepan and leave to simmer on a low heat for 20 minutes, stirring occasionally and scraping the bottom of the pan to ensure the mixture doesn't burn. Set it aside to cool, then cover with cling film and chill in the refrigerator for 1 hour.

Spoon the chilled mixture into kulfi or jelly moulds and place in the freezer for at least 5 hours.

To serve, unmould each kulfi on to a dessert plate (first running the mould under a lukewarm tap for a few seconds, to help you remove the kulfi easily). Decorate the kulfis with more raspberries.

# *summer fruit knickerbocker glory*

Served in a tall sundae glass, and thought to have originated (quite surprisingly so) in the UK during the 1930s, the knickerbocker glory is a true classic. In the traditional version (see also page 126 for a decadent chocolate knickerbocker) layers of fresh fruit, cream and ice cream are combined to create a delicious cold tower of taste sensations. For me, a knickerbocker glory perfectly evokes memories of long, hot, lazy summer holidays in the garden.

### *makes 4 individual servings*

### *for the fruit coulis*
300g assorted summer fruits, washed
1 tablespoon caster sugar
1 tablespoon cornflour

### *for the strawberries & cream ice cream*
300g strawberries, washed and hulled
1 teaspoon lemon juice
100ml whole milk
200ml double cream
6 large free-range egg yolks
150g caster sugar
1 tablespoon clotted cream
1 teaspoon freshly ground black pepper

### *for the Bourbon vanilla ice cream*
1 vanilla pod
500ml double cream
400ml whole milk
180g caster sugar
6 large free-range egg yolks
1 tablespoon Madagascan vanilla extract

### *for assembling*
150ml double or whipping cream
1 teaspoon caster sugar
200g fresh strawberries, washed and hulled
200g fresh raspberries, washed

First make the fruit coulis. Place the fruits in a saucepan over a low-to-medium heat and bring to a simmer. Continue to simmer gently for 10 minutes or so until the fruit begins to soften. Add the sugar, continue to simmer, stirring occasionally until the sugar is completely dissolved. Add the cornflour to thicken the coulis and mix until fully combined.

Strain the coulis through a fine sieve into a bowl, to remove any pips, and set aside to cool in the fridge.

Using the recipes on pages 48 and 149 respectively, make a fresh batch of the Bourbon Vanilla and the Strawberries & Cream ice cream. Decant them into separate containers and leave in the freezer to set solid.

Remove both ice creams from the freezer about 15 minutes before serving so that they can soften slightly.

Add the sugar to the double/whipping cream and whip the cream until it forms soft peaks.

Prepare each Knickerbocker Glory in a tall glass. Line the glass with fruit coulis, turning the glass to coat it with the coulis, and fill the bottom with a handful of strawberries and raspberries, followed by a generous helping of coulis, and layered scoops of vanilla and strawberry ice cream. Top off with more fruit coulis, whipped cream and more fresh fruit. Serve with a long sundae spoon.

# *summer fruits ice lollies*

**A real summer treat to help you cool off in style, these ice lollies can be made with or without a dash of fruity Pimm's No. 1 (or other similar fruit cup). For something really different try freezing the mixture in an ice cube tray and serving the cubes in a tall glass of prosecco.**

handful of fresh strawberries and/or
    raspberries, washed and hulled
few sprigs fresh mint, leaves only
zest of 1 orange
3 tablespoons cold water
400ml lemonade
1 teaspoon Pimm's No. 1 or similar (optional)

Cut the strawberries in half. Place a couple of strawberry halves, a few mint leaves and a little orange zest in each lolly mould.

In a mixing bowl or jug, quickly mix together the water and lemonade (and Pimm's if using) until fully combined. (Speed is desirable here, so that the lemonade does not go flat.)

Pour the liquid into each ice lolly mould until about three-quarters full. Insert the lolly stick and lid and freeze for 3 hours, or until fully frozen.

To remove the lollies, dip the moulds briefly into a bowl of hot water, then carefully remove the lollies and enjoy.

*citru*

This chapter focuses on ice creams, sorbets and desserts made using different citrus fruits of all variety from lemons and limes to oranges.

The effect of citric acid on lactose e.g. milk and cream, can often make it difficult to use fresh lemon, orange and lime juice in ice cream making, but by carefully following these recipes you shouldn't go far wrong. Remember that by using too much fresh citrus fruit juice and not whisking vigorously enough then you will be likely to burn the milk and cream in your recipe which will leave you with lumpy and sour tasting ice cream. Of course, if you don't use enough citrus juice your ice cream may be left dull tasting and under flavoured.

From sweet lemon posset, orange marmalade on burnt toast to alcoholic favourites such as gin and tonic sorbet, the recipes in this chapter have been inspired by everything from my favourite cocktail to my favourite breakfast. My lemon squid ink is a real piece of theatre, bold in texture, taste and colour and with a strong aromatic aroma, it's a perfect example of just how multi-sensory ice cream can be. There's no letting up in other flavour's either, here are some of my boldest flavours to suit a range of different palettes, hopefully you'll agree.

## A citrus pouring syrup

To create a tart, yet sweet citrus syrup, bursting with flavour and perfect for lavishly pouring all over your ice cream or sorbets, finely grate the zest of 1 fresh lemon, 1 fresh orange and 1 fresh lime; add the juice of each; place in a saucepan and cover with caster sugar (100g should be adequate); add 5 tablespoons of cold water; cover and heat for 10 minutes on a low heat. Remove the lid and vigorously stir the juice and zest; by now the sugar should have dissolved and the mixture begun to thicken. Continue to heat without the lid for a further 10 minutes. Set the saucepan aside to cool, then pour the liquid fruit into a blender and purée on full speed for a few seconds. Ensure that there are no clumps of zest remaining; if there are, blitz again. Decant the puréed mixture into a bowl, cover and set in the fridge to chill until required.

# lemon posset ice cream

Such a simple, easy pudding, full of sweet, tantalising citrus flavour, lemon posset works fantastically well in ice cream. The acidity of the dish is somewhat mellowed by the cream in the ice cream base.

1 unwaxed lemon
250ml double cream
150g purchased lemon curd
3 tablespoons orange blossom honey
250ml fresh yoghurt
150g caster sugar
1 large free-range egg

Carefully and finely grate the zest of the unwaxed lemon into a mixing bowl, combine with double cream and whisk until the mixture is thick enough to coat the back of a spoon.

Fold the lemon curd and honey into the cream base mix, then stir in the remaining ingredients before decanting into a saucepan.

Gently heat the mixture over a low heat for about 10 minutes to allow it to thicken and for the flavours infuse.

Pour the mixture into a bowl or large jug and set aside to chill in the refrigerator for about 1 hour.

Pour the chilled ice cream mixture into your ice cream maker and set it to churn. Once it has finished churning, decant the partially frozen ice cream into a freezer-friendly container and leave it in the freezer to set solid.

If you do not have an ice cream maker, follow the instructions on page 25.

Remove the ice cream from the freezer about 15 minutes before serving so that it can soften slightly. Serve it in a meringue nest or in a sundae glass.

# lemon meringue ice cream

Based on my favourite homemade lemon meringue pie, this sweet, sharp and flavoursome ice cream is simple to make using purchased lemon curd, and the velvety texture of the base contrasts beautifully with bits of crunchy meringue. For an additional flavour contrast, serve it with Bourbon Vanilla Ice Cream (see page 48).

75g meringues, roughly crushed
5 free-range egg yolks
150g vanilla sugar (see page 39)
250ml whole milk
250ml double cream
a dash of lemon juice
1 teaspoon vanilla extract
100g purchased lemon curd

Following the recipe on page 271, bake a fresh batch of meringue nests (but simply spoon the mixture on to the baking tray, rather than forming nests). Crush several of these, to make 75g, and set aside until ready.

Place the egg yolks and sugar in a mixing bowl and beat the mixture until it forms a thick, pale and smooth paste.

Pour the milk, cream and lemon juice into a saucepan, along with the vanilla extract and lemon curd, and bring to a simmer. Let the mixture simmer for about 10 minutes, stirring constantly, to allow the flavours to infuse fully.

Stir in the egg and sugar mixture and continue to heat, stirring constantly, until the mixture is thick enough to coat the back of a spoon.

Pour the mixture into a bowl or large jug and leave it to cool at room temperature. Then cover it with cling film and place it in the refrigerator to chill for at least 1 hour.

Pour the chilled mixture into your ice cream maker and set it to churn. Once it has finished churning, decant the partially frozen ice cream into a freezer-friendly container and leave it in the freezer to set solid.

If you do not have an ice cream maker, follow the instructions on page 25.

Remove the ice cream from the freezer about 15 minutes before serving so that it can soften slightly.

# marmalade and burnt toast ice cream

A thick spreading of rough-cut orange marmalade served over slightly burnt toast is unequivocally breakfast in a bite, so why not exploit this inspired combination of flavours and textures to create a treat that you can enjoy, not at the breakfast table while still half asleep, but at any time of the day? All you need is a scoop of this ice cream!

250ml double cream
250ml whole milk
50g caster sugar
300g orange marmalade, preferably organic
1 slice of burnt toast, blitzed into fine
   breadcrumbs
3 tablespoons (or to taste) fresh orange juice

In a blender, mix together the cream, milk, sugar, marmalade and breadcrumbs. Add orange juice to taste and blend to a smooth consistency.

Transfer the mixture to a medium-sized saucepan and cook gently for 10–15 minutes over a medium heat, stirring occasionally and being careful not to boil the mixture, in order to prevent the cream from curdling.

Pour the mixture into a bowl or large jug and leave it to cool at room temperature. Then cover it with cling film and place it in the refrigerator to chill for at least 1 hour.

Pour the chilled mixture into your ice cream maker and set it to churn. Once it has finished churning, decant the partially frozen ice cream into a freezer-friendly container and leave it in the freezer to set solid.

If you do not have an ice cream maker, follow the instructions on page 25.

Remove the ice cream from the freezer about 15 minutes before serving so that it can soften slightly.

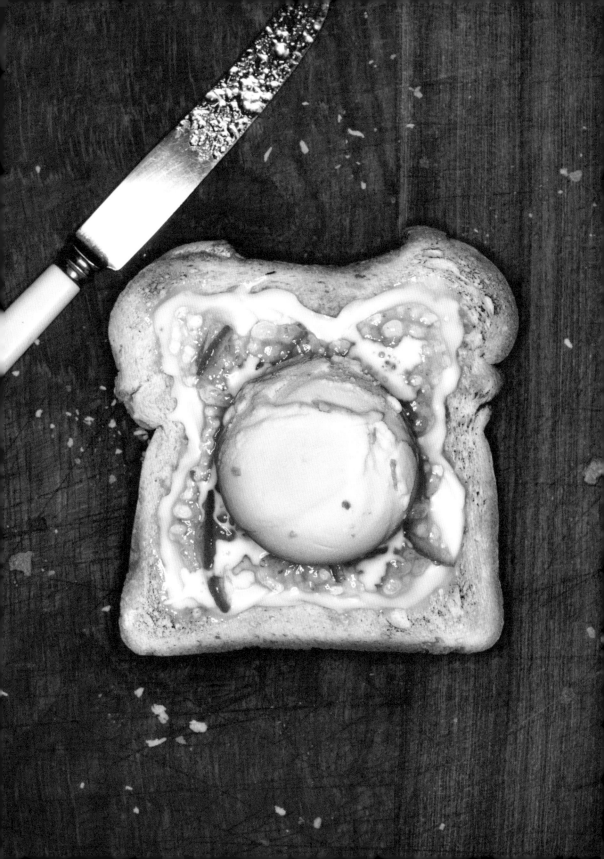

# key lime pie ice cream

A much-loved dessert in the United States, Key lime pie is a simple custard pie similar to lemon meringue pie. Although traditionally made from the small limes grown on the Florida Keys (islands off that state's southern coast), it can be made with any limes – as can this fresh-tasting ice cream. Lemon juice and a hint of vanilla extract help to create a full, complex flavour.

2 limes
2 lemons
100g caster sugar, plus 2 tablespoons
250ml whole milk
200g mascarpone
1 teaspoon vanilla extract
1 sheet of pectin or gelatine (20–25g)
50g digestive biscuits, crushed

Begin by making a lime and lemon mash: halve the fruits and scrape out the flesh and juices into a saucepan, then cover this with 2 tablespoons of sugar and gently heat for 5–10 minutes, stirring constantly to ensure the fruit doesn't burn.

Once all of the sugar has dissolved, set the mixture aside to cool, then pour into a blender or food processor and purée until there are no lumps. Push the purée through a sieve to remove any seeds and set aside for use later.

In a saucepan gently heat the milk, sugar, vanilla and mascarpone for 5 minutes, gently stirring; do not allow to boil. Reduce the heat and submerge the gelatine sheet, then gradually increase the heat and continue to stir until fully dissolved.

Once dissolved, the mixture should begin to thicken up enough to coat the back of a spoon. At this point fold in the purée and vigorously whisk to prevent the mixture from burning. Continue to heat and stir for a few more minutes, then remove from the heat.

Pour the mixture into a bowl or large jug and leave it to cool at room temperature. Then cover it with cling film and place it in the refrigerator to chill for at least 1 hour.

Pour the chilled mixture into your ice cream maker and set it to churn. Once it has finished churning, decant the partially frozen ice cream into a freezer-friendly container, stir in the crushed digestive biscuits and leave it in the freezer to set solid.

If you do not have an ice cream maker, follow the instructions on page 25, adding the crushed digestive biscuits before placing the ice cream in the freezer for the first time.

Remove the ice cream from the freezer about 15 minutes before serving so that it can soften slightly.

# orange, basil and bay sorbet

A somewhat unusual-sounding mixture of ingredients which work perfectly together to create a very aromatic and delicately balanced sorbet, perfect for cooling off with on a warm summer's evening.

175g caster sugar
100ml water
30ml lemon juice
500ml orange juice
10 fresh basil leaves
2 fresh bay leaves

Pour the sugar and water into a pan and slowly bring to the boil, stirring the mixture until the sugar has fully dissolved and the mixture begins to thicken into a syrup. Remove from the heat and set aside.

Pour the juices into a blender or food processor, add the basil leaves and blitz until all of the basil leaves have been adequately blended.

Pour the mixture into a bowl, cover with cling film and place in the refrigerator for 1 hour to allow the flavours to infuse.

Remove the orange juice mixture from the fridge, add it to the sugar syrup, submerge the bay leaves and return the pan to the heat. Continue to heat, stirring occasionally, for about 10 minutes, or until the mixture is thick enough to coat the back of a spoon.

Pass the mixture through a fine sieve into a bowl or large jug (discarding the bay leaves) and set it aside to cool. Then cover it with cling film and place it in the refrigerator to chill for at least 1 hour.

Pour the chilled mixture into your ice cream maker and set it to churn. Once it has finished churning, decant the partially frozen sorbet into a freezer-friendly container and leave it in the freezer to set solid.

If you do not have an ice cream maker, follow the instructions on page 25.

Remove the sorbet from the freezer about 15 minutes before serving so that it can soften slightly.

# *orange sorbet*

This is very simple and enormously refreshing, made using fresh orange juice, water, sugar and just a hint of lemon juice to add a little zing. If you like this one, do also try the intensely sharp Blood Orange Sorbet on page 183.

200g caster sugar
325ml water
400ml orange juice
1 teaspoon lemon juice

Pour the sugar and water into a saucepan and bring to a simmer over a medium heat. Cook, stirring, until the sugar has fully dissolved and the mixture has thickened to a syrupy consistency, then continue to simmer for a further 5 minutes.

Reduce the heat to low, add the orange and lemon juice and whisk until fully combined. Remove from the heat.

Pour the mixture into a bowl or large jug and leave it to cool at room temperature. Then cover it with cling film and place it in the refrigerator to chill and for the flavours to infuse fully for at least 1 hour.

Pour the chilled mixture into your ice cream maker and set it to churn. Once it has finished churning, decant the partially frozen sorbet into a freezer-friendly container and leave it in the freezer to set solid.

If you do not have an ice cream maker, follow the instructions on page 25.

Remove the sorbet from the freezer about 15 minutes before serving so that it can soften slightly.

# lemon and squid ink ice cream

Currently a favourite ice cream flavour in Japan, squid ink may not have instant appeal to most Western palates. My own lemon and squid ink ice cream, however, is inspired by traditional Venetian cookery, where dishes are delicately flavoured and simply stand on their own, with just one or two distinctive ingredients added to enhance the food experience. Lemon not only helps to bring out the complex flavour of the squid ink and lactic milk and cream flavours, it also provides a strong, perfumed scent.

200ml whole milk
100ml squid ink
350ml double cream
1 tablespoon lemon juice
5 large free-range egg yolks
120g caster sugar

Pour the milk and squid ink into a mixing bowl, cover with cling film and leave in the fridge to chill and infuse overnight.

Pour the infused milk, the cream and the lemon juice into a saucepan; place over a low-to-medium heat and bring to a simmer, stirring occasionally. Cover the pan, turn the heat all the way down and leave for 3 hours to allow flavour maturation to take place.

Meanwhile, place the egg yolks and sugar in a mixing bowl and whisk together until you have a pale, thick and glossy paste. Set aside until the milk mixture is ready.

Bring the milk mixture back up to a simmer, then gradually pour it into the egg mixture, whisking all the time, until it is well incorporated.

Return the mixture to the saucepan and cook for about 10 minutes on a low-to-medium heat, stirring constantly, until it has thickened enough to coat the back of the spoon. Remove from heat.

Pour the mixture into a bowl or large jug and leave it to cool at room temperature. Use an electric whisk to aerate the mixture, then cover it with cling film and place it in the refrigerator to chill for at least 1 hour.

Pour the chilled mixture into your ice cream maker and set it to churn. Once it has finished churning, decant the partially frozen ice cream into a freezer-friendly container and leave it in the freezer to set solid.

If you do not have an ice cream maker, follow the instructions on page 25.

Remove the ice cream from the freezer about 15 minutes before serving so that it can soften slightly. Use a melon baller or similar to scoop small balls of the ice cream into shot glasses.

# *blood orange sorbet*

This refreshing sorbet is the grown-up version of the Orange Sorbet on page 179, offering a perfect balance of tangy, sharp orange and sweetness in every mouthful.

200g caster sugar
400ml water
400ml blood orange juice
1 teaspoon lemon juice

Pour the sugar and water into a saucepan and bring to a simmer over a medium heat. Cook, stirring, until the sugar has fully dissolved and the mixture has thickened to a syrupy consistency, then continue to simmer for a further 5 minutes.

Reduce the heat to low, add the orange and lemon juice and whisk until fully combined. Remove from the heat.

Pour the mixture into a bowl or large jug and leave it to cool at room temperature. Then cover it with cling film and place it in the refrigerator to chill and for the flavours to infuse fully for at least 1 hour.

Pour the chilled mixture into your ice cream maker and set it to churn. Once it has finished churning, decant the partially frozen sorbet into a freezer-friendly container and leave it in the freezer to set solid.

If you do not have an ice cream maker, follow the instructions on page 25.

Remove the sorbet from the freezer about 15 minutes before serving so that it can soften slightly.

# lemon sorbet

A classic sorbet, and for good reason, lemon sorbet has a beautifully crisp and clean flavour. The use of gelatine in this recipe, as with the Beetroot Sorbet (page 229), gives the sorbet greater body and stability, making it easy to scoop. The sorbet will last up to three months when kept covered in the freezer.

200g caster sugar
325ml water
250ml lemonade
1 teaspoon lime juice
zest of 1 lemon
1 sheet gelatine (20–25g)

Pour the caster sugar and water into a saucepan and place over a medium heat for about 3–5 minutes, stirring, until all the sugar has dissolved and the liquid becomes syrupy. Remove from the heat and set aside to cool.

Once cool, add the lemonade, lime juice and lemon zest to the syrup and whisk all of the ingredients together until fully combined.

Now return the pan to a gentle heat. While the liquid simmers, soften the gelatine sheet in a cup of cold water for 5 minutes, then squeeze out the excess water and add the gelatine to the sorbet mixture.

Return the mixture to a medium heat for 5 minutes to ensure that the gelatine has completely dissolved, then remove the saucepan from the heat.

Pour the mixture into a bowl or large jug and leave it to cool at room temperature. Then cover it with cling film and place it in the refrigerator to chill for at least 1 hour.

Pour the chilled mixture into your ice cream maker and set it to churn. Once it has finished churning, decant the partially frozen sorbet into a freezer-friendly container and leave it in the freezer to set solid.

If you do not have an ice cream maker, follow the instructions on page 25.

Remove the sorbet from the freezer about 15 minutes before serving so that it can soften slightly.

# *mojito ice lolly*

A dash of lime, a sprig of mint and a lot of rum – all of the constituent parts of the perfect mojito, a favourite Cuban cocktail which rose to popularity in the nineteenth century. Just like the cocktail, the ice lolly version does not disappoint. It is best served on a stick or in a tall drink as flavoured ice cubes.

*makes up to 12 ice lollies*
*or 24 ice cubes*

juice and zest of 8 limes (150ml)
150ml water
a handful of fresh mint leaves
75g caster sugar
2 tablespoons light rum

Pour the lime juice and water into a bowl, add the zest and the mint leaves, cover with cling film and leave in the fridge for up 1 hour to allow the flavours to infuse.

Remove the bowl from the fridge, stir in the sugar and rum, re-cover and return to the fridge for another hour.

Transfer the mixture to a saucepan and place on a low heat to dissolve the sugar. Once dissolved, remove from the heat and set aside to cool. Strain it through a fine sieve to remove the mint leaves.

Whisk the cooled mixture to ensure that all of the ingredients are thoroughly mixed, then pour into your ice lolly moulds or ice cube trays and place in the freezer to set solid.

herbs
and spices

*herbs*

This chapter focuses on ice creams and other desserts made using herbs and spices of various kinds, from everyday ones such as mint, nutmeg and cinnamon to more unusual ones such as liquorice and wasabi. Spices give ice cream a paradoxically warming character, especially suitable for the winter months.

## A spiced pouring syrup

As an alternative to making a spicy flavour of ice cream, you can use spices to make a delicious syrup for pouring over vanilla ice cream, for example. The recipe that follows can also be used as a mulling syrup with wine or cider. It makes about 250ml.

Place 250g of caster sugar, 3 oranges (halved) and 2 teaspoons each of ground nutmeg, ground allspice and ground cloves in a saucepan, along with 2 cinnamon sticks and 1 litre of water. Bring to a gentle simmer and let simmer for 10–15 minutes, stirring almost continuously until the sugar and spices have fully dissolved. Now increase the heat and bring to the boil for 5–10 minutes, or until the mixture has thickened to a syrupy consistency. Set aside to cool, then set in the fridge to chill for an hour. Decant the chilled syrup into two sterilised bottles and return to the refrigerator, where it will keep for two weeks. Alternatively, you can use the syrup itself as a Christmas sorbet, leaving it in the freezer to set solid before serving it in generous-sized scoops.

# caramelised apple pie ice cream

**My ice cream version of a classic autumn dessert. Warming cinnamon, sweet, sharp and mellow apples, and rich double cream help make this ice cream extremely comforting. Best served with a generous dollop of clotted cream.**

500g cooking apples, cored and peeled or left
    unpeeled, as you like
3 tablespoons light brown sugar
250ml whole milk
250ml double cream
2 teaspoons ground cinnamon
6 free-range egg yolks
200g caster sugar
50g digestive biscuits, roughly crushed

First caramelise the apples. Pre-heat the oven to 190°C/Gas Mark 5. Roughly chop all of the apples and carefully lay them out evenly on a baking tray; cover with the light brown sugar and sprinkle a few teaspoons of cold water on top. Bake the apples for about 15 minutes, or until they are golden and coated with the melted brown sugar. Set aside to cool for use later.

Now make the ice cream base. Pour the milk and cream into a saucepan and place over a medium heat; bring to a simmer, stirring constantly to stop the mixture from burning. Once it is simmering add the ground cinnamon. Remove from the heat and set aside, remembering to stir occasionally.

Place the egg yolks and sugar in a mixing bowl and whisk together until you have a pale, thick and glossy paste.

Bring the milk mixture back up to a simmer, then gradually pour it into the egg mixture, whisking all the time, until it is well incorporated.

Return the mixture to the saucepan and cook for about 10 minutes on a low-to-medium heat, stirring constantly, until it has thickened enough to coat the back of the spoon. Stir in half of the caramelised apples and remove from heat.

Pour the mixture into a bowl or large jug and leave it to cool at room temperature. Then place it in the refrigerator to chill for at least 1 hour.

Pour the chilled mixture into your ice cream maker and set it to churn. Once it has finished churning, decant the partially frozen ice cream into a freezer-friendly container. Stir in the crumbled digestive biscuits and remaining caramelised apples and place the ice cream in the freezer to set solid.

If you do not have an ice cream maker, follow the instructions on page 25.

Remove the ice cream from the freezer about 15 minutes before serving so that it can soften slightly.

# *mint chocolate chip ice cream*

**Arguably the most popular flavour in the cabinets of our ice cream parlours, 'mint choc chip' packs a hefty punch of flavour. (It's not my own favourite, but maybe I ate too much of it in my teens.) For the chips in this recipe it's best to chop up a few bars of your favourite dark chocolate. Add a dash of crème de menthe for a gorgeous green colour.**

250ml whole milk
400ml double cream
150g caster sugar
80g fresh mint leaves (roughly 2 handfuls)
5 large free-range egg yolks
50g chocolate chips

In a saucepan gently heat the milk, the cream and half of the sugar. Bring to a simmer, stirring constantly, then add the mint leaves. Remove from heat and allow flavours to infuse for 1 hour.

Pass the mixture through a fine sieve into another saucepan; discard the mint leaves.

Place the egg yolks and remaining sugar in a mixing bowl and whisk together until you have a pale, thick and glossy paste.

Bring the milk mixture back up to a simmer, then gradually pour it into the egg mixture, whisking all the time, until it is well incorporated.

Return the mixture to the saucepan and cook for about 10 minutes on a low-to-medium heat, stirring constantly, until it has thickened enough to coat the back of the spoon. Remove from heat.

Pour the mixture into a bowl or large jug and leave to cool at room temperature. Once cool, stir in the chocolate chips, then place the ice cream in the refrigerator to chill for at least 1 hour.

Pour the chilled ice cream mixture into your ice cream maker and set it to churn. Once it has finished churning, decant the partially frozen ice cream into a freezer-friendly container and leave it in the freezer to set solid.

If you do not have an ice cream maker, follow the instructions on page 25.

Remove the ice cream from the freezer about 15 minutes before serving so that it can soften slightly.

# *spiced plum ice cream*

Using up the last of the season's overripe plums and adding some winter spices produces an ice cream which is complex on various levels, delicate, but powerful, surprisingly warming and quintessentially festive.

400g plums, stones removed, but unpeeled
a dash of lemon juice
200ml whole milk
100ml double cream
3 large free-range egg yolks
150g caster sugar
1 teaspoon ground cinnamon
1 teaspoon ground nutmeg

In a blender or food processor, blend the plums, along with the lemon juice and a few tablespoons of water, until the mixture is completely smooth.

Pour the milk and cream into a saucepan and place over a low-to-medium heat. Bring to a simmer, stirring frequently to ensure that the mixture doesn't burn; do not allow it to boil. Let it simmer for about 5 minutes, then remove from the heat and set aside, remembering to stir occasionally.

Place the egg yolks and sugar in a mixing bowl and whisk together until you have a pale, thick and glossy paste.

Bring the milk mixture back up to a simmer, then gradually pour it into the egg mixture, whisking all the time, until it is well incorporated.

Return the mixture to the saucepan and stir in the plums, cinnamon and nutmeg; mix well to ensure that the ingredients are well combined. Cook for about 10 minutes on a low-to-medium heat, stirring constantly, until it has thickened enough to coat the back of the spoon. Remove from heat.

Pour the mixture into a bowl or large jug and leave it to cool at room temperature. Then cover it with cling film and place it in the refrigerator to chill for at least 1 hour.

Pour the chilled mixture into your ice cream maker and set it to churn. Once it has finished churning, decant the partially frozen ice cream into a freezer-friendly container and leave it in the freezer to set solid.

If you do not have an ice cream maker, follow the instructions on page 25.

Remove the ice cream from the freezer about 15 minutes before serving so that it can soften slightly.

# *wasabi ice cream*

Wasabi is a spicy, powerful root plant also known as Japanese horseradish. Available fresh or as a powder, wasabi can be used to make a quite brilliant ice cream, in which the pungency of this flavouring overrides the sweetness of the ice cream base to create a well-balanced, savoury taste. Best served with smoked fish or gamey meats, or before the meal as an amuse-bouche, this unusual ice cream is sure to impress.

200ml whole milk
250ml double cream
5 large free-range egg yolks
150g caster sugar
2 tablespoons ground wasabi

Pour the milk and cream into a saucepan and place over a low-to-medium heat. Bring to a simmer, stirring frequently to ensure that the mixture doesn't burn; do not allow it to boil. Let it simmer for about 5 minutes, then remove from the heat and set aside, remembering to stir occasionally.

Place the egg yolks and sugar in a mixing bowl and whisk together until you have a pale, thick and glossy paste.

Bring the milk mixture back up to a simmer, then gradually pour it into the egg mixture, whisking all the time, until it is well incorporated.

Return the mixture to the saucepan, add the wasabi and cook for about 10 minutes on a low-to-medium heat, stirring constantly, until it has thickened enough to coat the back of the spoon. Remove from heat.

Pour the mixture into a bowl or large jug and leave it to cool at room temperature. Then place it in the refrigerator to chill for at least 1 hour.

Remove it from the fridge and whisk for about 5 minutes using an electric whisk; this will ensure that the ingredients have fully combined and will add a small amount of air to the ice cream, helping to make it smooth.

Pour the chilled ice cream mixture into your ice cream maker and set it to churn. Once it has finished churning, decant the partially frozen ice cream into a freezer-friendly container and leave it in the freezer to set solid.

If you do not have an ice cream maker, follow the instructions on page 25.

Remove the ice cream from the freezer about 15 minutes before serving so that it can soften slightly.

# ginger and honey ice cream

**Two popular flavours are combined in this rich ice cream: the strong, smoky flavour of the ginger is balanced beautifully with the delicate flavour of honey – all enhanced by the sweetness of the ice cream base. The use of different kinds of honey can provide subtle but interesting differences.**

300ml double cream
250ml whole milk
2 teaspoons ground ginger
4 large free-range egg yolks
100g caster sugar
100g clear (runny) honey
1 teaspoon crystallised ginger

Pour the cream and milk into a medium saucepan; add the ground ginger. Gently heat the mixture almost, but not quite, to boiling point, stirring almost constantly to ensure that it doesn't burn; do not allow it to boil. Let it simmer for about 5 minutes, then remove from the heat and set aside, remembering to stir occasionally.

Place the egg yolks and sugar in a mixing bowl and whisk together until you have a pale, thick and glossy paste.

Bring the milk mixture back up to a simmer, then gradually pour it into the egg mixture, whisking all the time, until it is well incorporated.

Return the mixture to the saucepan, pour in the honey and cook for about 10 minutes on a low-to-medium heat, stirring constantly, until the mixture has thickened enough to coat the back of the spoon. Remove from heat.

Pour the mixture into a bowl or large jug and leave it to cool at room temperature. Then place it in the refrigerator to chill for at least 1 hour.

Mix the crystallised ginger into the chilled ice cream mixture.

Pour the mixture into your ice cream maker and set it to churn. Once it has finished churning, decant the partially frozen ice cream into a freezer-friendly container and leave it in the freezer to set solid.

If you do not have an ice cream maker, follow the instructions on page 25.

Remove the ice cream from the freezer about 15 minutes before serving so that it can soften slightly.

Serve with fresh fruit or Toffee Syrup (see page 95).

# *mixed spice winter ice cream*

**An aromatic blend of cinnamon, nutmeg, allspice, cloves and other ingredients, mixed spice here combines beautifully with mincemeat, ginger and the caramel notes of brown sugar to make this the quintessential Christmas ice cream, bursting with flavour. Why not serve it as an alternative to Christmas pudding?**

400ml double cream
250ml whole milk
2 teaspoons ground ginger
1 teaspoon mixed spice
6 large free-range egg yolks
120g light brown sugar
2 tablespoons mincemeat
1 tablespoon mixed peel

Pour the cream and milk into a medium saucepan; add the ground ginger and mixed spice and place over a low-to-medium heat. Bring to a simmer, stirring frequently to ensure that the mixture doesn't burn; do not allow it to boil. Let it simmer for about 5 minutes, then remove from the heat and set aside, remembering to stir occasionally.

Place the egg yolks and sugar in a mixing bowl and whisk together until you have a pale, thick and glossy paste.

Bring the milk mixture back up to a simmer, then gradually pour it into the egg mixture, whisking all the time, until it is well incorporated.

Return the mixture to the saucepan and cook for about 10 minutes on a low-to-medium heat, stirring constantly, until it has thickened enough to coat the back of the spoon. Remove from heat.

Pour the mixture into a bowl or large jug and leave it to cool at room temperature. Then place it in the refrigerator to chill for at least 1 hour.

Pour the chilled ice cream mixture into your ice cream maker and set it to churn. Once it has finished churning, decant the partially frozen ice cream into a freezer-friendly container, stir in the mincemeat and mixed peel and leave it in the freezer to set solid.

If you do not have an ice cream maker, follow the instructions on page 25.

Remove the ice cream from the freezer about 15 minutes before serving so that it can soften slightly.

# chilli and lime sorbet

This refreshing sorbet packs a punch; initially slightly tart, the flavour then develops on the tongue with a fiery chilli finish and a hint of fresh basil. It is best served in small portions – perhaps as an amuse-bouche, as a palate cleanser or as a light summer dessert.

1 fresh red chilli
zest and juice of 2 lemons
zest and juice of 2 limes
1 basil leaf, finely chopped
225g caster sugar
750ml water
zest of 1 orange

Using a sharp knife slice the chilli in half lengthways; remove and dispose of any seeds and chop the chilli into small pieces.

Put the chilli in a saucepan along with the lemon and lime zest and juice, the chopped basil, the sugar and the water; place over a low heat.

Continue to heat gently, stirring occasionally, until the sugar has completely dissolved; increase the heat slightly to bring the mixture close to the boil; allow to simmer for 5 minutes, then remove from the heat.

Pour the mixture into a bowl or large jug and leave it to cool at room temperature. It will begin to thicken slightly. Then place it in the refrigerator to chill for at least 1 hour.

Pour the chilled sorbet mixture into your ice cream maker and set it to churn. Once it has finished churning, decant the partially frozen sorbet into a freezer-friendly container and leave it in the freezer to set solid.

If you do not have an ice cream maker, follow the instructions on page 25.

Remove the sorbet from the freezer about 15 minutes before serving so that it can soften slightly.

Place a small scoop in a shot glass; top it with a little orange zest.

# clove and lavender ice cream

**Traditionally used in Indian cuisine and in Christmas cookery, thanks largely to its earthy, aromatic and pungent flavour, clove also works well with the lactic flavour of ice cream. Combining it with lavender creates a palate-pleasing sensation of different complementary flavours.**

250ml whole milk
400ml double cream
6 free-range egg yolks
125g caster sugar or lavender sugar
   (see page 39)
2 teaspoons ground cloves
2 teaspoons lavender essence

Pour the milk and cream into a saucepan and place over a low-to-medium heat. Bring to a simmer, stirring frequently to ensure that the mixture doesn't burn; do not allow it to boil. Let it simmer for about 5 minutes, then remove from the heat and set aside, remembering to stir occasionally.

Place the egg yolks and sugar in a mixing bowl and whisk together until you have a pale, thick and glossy paste.

Bring the milk mixture back up to a simmer, then gradually pour it into the egg mixture, whisking all the time, until it is well incorporated.

Return the mixture to the saucepan and cook for about 10 minutes on a low-to-medium heat, stirring constantly, until it has thickened enough to coat the back of the spoon. Add the ground cloves and lavender essence and cook on a low heat, stirring frequently, for another 10 minutes to allow the flavours to infuse.

Remove the mixture from heat. Pour it into a bowl or large jug and leave it to cool at room temperature. Then place it in the refrigerator to chill for at least 1 hour.

Pour the chilled mixture into your ice cream maker and set it to churn. Once it has finished churning, decant the partially frozen ice cream into a freezer-friendly container and leave it in the freezer to set solid.

If you do not have an ice cream maker, follow the instructions on page 25.

Remove the ice cream from the freezer about 15 minutes before serving so that it can soften slightly.

Serve this ice cream, if you like, with a generous helping of double cream.

# chocolate, chilli and rosemary kulfi

These three powerful flavours, added to a rich, creamy, kulfi base, acquire a peppery, aromatic caramel-type character. When served in small scoops or in kulfi or even jelly moulds, this dessert makes an impressive conclusion to a meal.

$1/_2$ teaspoon cornflour
300ml condensed milk
200ml double cream
100g light brown sugar
1 sprig rosemary
1 teaspoon ground chilli
1 tablespoon cocoa powder

Mix the cornflour with the condensed milk in a saucepan. Place it over a low-to-medium heat and bring it to a simmer, stirring constantly to prevent it from boiling.

Once it has reached a simmer, add the double cream, sugar, rosemary, chilli and cocoa powder, stirring well with a whisk to ensure all of the ingredients are well combined. Continue to heat until all of the sugar has dissolved.

Remove the pan from the heat. and set aside to cool. Remove the rosemary sprig.

Use an electric whisk for a couple of minutes, at high speed, to ensure that the mixture is entirely free of lumps – a common occurrence when using condensed milk.

Pour the kulfi mixture into a bowl or large jug, cover it with cling film and place it in the refrigerator to chill for at least 1 hour.

Pour the chilled mixture into your ice cream maker and set it to churn. Once it has finished churning, decant the partially frozen kulfi into the kulfi or jelly moulds and put into the freezer to set solid.

If you do not have an ice cream maker, follow the instructions on page 25.

To serve, unmould each kulfi on to a dessert plate (first running the mould under a lukewarm tap for a few seconds, to help you remove the kulfi easily).

# *gingerbread ice cream*

**Biscuits made of gingerbread cut into a variety of shapes have been a popular delicacy in England at least since the time of Queen Elizabeth I, when they were enjoyed by her courtiers. In Victorian times the gingerbread man made his appearance (along with the children's story of a gingerbread man who escaped the jaws of a fox). This ice cream, laced with ginger, cinnamon, nutmeg and cloves, evokes the distinctive, spicy flavour of this perennial treat.**

250ml whole milk
300ml double cream
2 teaspoons ground ginger
1 teaspoon cinnamon
1 teaspoon nutmeg
1 teaspoon ground cloves
4 large free-range egg yolks
100g caster sugar

Pour the milk and cream into a saucepan, along with the spices, and place over a low-to-medium heat. Bring to a simmer, stirring frequently to ensure that the mixture doesn't burn; do not allow it to boil. Let it simmer for about 5 minutes, then remove from the heat and set aside, remembering to stir occasionally.

Place the egg yolks and sugar in a mixing bowl and whisk together until you have a pale, thick and glossy paste.

Bring the milk mixture back up to a simmer, then gradually pour it into the egg mixture, whisking all the time, until it is well incorporated.

Return the mixture to the saucepan and cook for about 10 minutes on a low-to-medium heat, stirring constantly, until it has thickened enough to coat the back of the spoon. Remove from heat.

Pour the mixture into a bowl or large jug and leave it to cool at room temperature. Then cover it with cling film and place it in the refrigerator to chill for at least 1 hour.

Pour the chilled mixture into your ice cream maker and set it to churn. Once it has finished churning, decant the partially frozen ice cream into a freezer-friendly container and leave it in the freezer to set solid.

If you do not have an ice cream maker, follow the instructions on page 25.

Remove the ice cream from the freezer about 15 minutes before serving so that it can soften slightly.

# botanical infusions

*botai*

This chapter focuses on ice creams made using infusions of various plant materials and extracts, ranging from conventional flavours such as rhubarb and rose water to less familiar territory, including ice creams made with matcha green tea and with olive oil which blur the distinction between sweet and savoury.

The perfect pairing for your botanical ice creams and sorbets has to be a traditional dandelion and burdock syrup. Simply heat 300ml water, 150g caster sugar, 1 teaspoon ground ginger, 1 teaspoon ground burdock root (you can buy this from wholefood and health food stores as well as numerous online retailers) and 1 teaspoon ground dandelion root, and bring to a rapid simmer for ten minutes, stirring occasionally. After ten minutes, set the syrup aside to cool and place in the fridge to chill. Serve poured over ice cream or sorbet or use as a delicious mixer with a slug of gin and tonic.

# *earl grey tea ice cream*

Carefully flavoured with bergamot, Earl Grey tea came into prominence in early nineteenth-century England, where it was seen as a more affordable alternative to expensive herbal Chinese teas. In this ice cream, the infusion of the tea into the milk and cream base creates a fragrant balance of flavours, helped along by a dash of fresh lemon juice to further enhance the flavour.

250ml whole milk
500ml double cream
3 Earl Grey tea bags
1 teaspoon lemon juice
150g caster sugar
5 large free-range egg yolks

Pour the milk and cream into a saucepan and place over a low-to-medium heat, Bring to a simmer, stirring frequently to ensure that the mixture doesn't burn; do not allow it to boil. Let it simmer for 5 minutes. Now reduce the heat and submerge the tea bags and add the lemon juice. Cover the pan, remove from the heat and set aside; let the mixture steep at room temperature for 2 hours to allow the tea's flavours to infuse in the milk and cream.

Meanwhile, place the sugar and egg yolks in a mixing bowl and whisk together, using a hand or electric mixer, until you have a pale, thick and glossy paste.

After 2 hours remove the teabags, return the saucepan to the heat and re-warm the tea-infused milk. Slowly pour the mixture into the egg yolks, whisking constantly until it is well incorporated.

Return the mixture to the saucepan and cook for about 10 minutes on a low-to-medium heat, stirring constantly, to prevent it from curdling, until it has thickened enough to coat the back of the spoon. Remove from heat.

Pour the mixture into a bowl or large jug and leave it to cool at room temperature. Then place it in the refrigerator to chill for at least 1 hour.

Following the manufacturer's instructions, pour the chilled ice cream mixture into your ice cream maker and set it to churn. Once it has finished churning, decant the partially frozen ice cream into a freezer-friendly container and leave it in the freezer to set solid.

If you do not have an ice cream maker, follow the instructions on page 25.

Remove the ice cream from the freezer about 15 minutes before serving so that it can soften slightly.

# rose water ice cream

**This ice cream recipe really stands out; it's very aromatic, thanks to the mingling of rose water, vanilla and honey. The delicately perfumed flavour notes evoke those of Turkish delight.**

250ml whole milk
125ml double cream
100g caster sugar
5 free-range egg yolks
2 tablespoons orange blossom honey
100ml rose water
1 teaspoon vanilla extract
a dash of lemon juice

Pour the milk and cream into a saucepan and place over a low-to-medium heat. Bring to a simmer, stirring frequently to ensure that the mixture doesn't burn; do not allow it to boil. Let it simmer for about 5 minutes, then remove from the heat and set aside, remembering to stir occasionally.

Place the sugar and egg yolks in a mixing bowl and whisk together, using a hand or electric mixer, until you have a pale, thick and glossy paste.

Bring the milk mixture back up to a simmer, then gradually pour it into the egg mixture, whisking all the time, until it is well incorporated.

Return the mixture to the saucepan. Carefully stir the honey, rose water and vanilla into the custard; add a dash of lemon juice to enhance the flavour of the rose water. Leave the custard to cook gently on a low-to-medium heat for a further 10 minutes to allow the flavours to mature and the consistency to thicken, stirring constantly, to prevent it from curdling, until it has thickened enough to coat the back of the spoon. Remove from heat.

Pour the mixture into a bowl or large jug and leave it to cool at room temperature. Then place it in the refrigerator to chill for at least 1 hour.

Following the manufacturer's instructions, pour the chilled ice cream mixture into your ice cream maker and set it to churn. Once it has finished churning, decant the partially frozen ice cream into a freezer-friendly container and leave it in the freezer to set solid.

If you do not have an ice cream maker, follow the instructions on page 25, whisking a total of 4 times, rather than 3.

Remove the ice cream from the freezer about 15 minutes before serving so that it can soften slightly.

# *matcha green tea ice cream*

**Bright green in colour, delicate in flavour and stuffed full of antioxidants and nutrients, matcha green tea, which comes from Japan, is a real super food. With the help of a little fresh lemon juice it makes a really fantastic, if somewhat unusual, ice cream.**

250ml whole milk
250ml double cream
125g caster sugar
5 large free-range egg yolks
1 tablespoon matcha green tea powder
? teaspoon fresh lemon juice

Pour the milk and cream into a saucepan and place over a low-to-medium heat. Bring to a simmer, stirring frequently to ensure that the mixture doesn't burn; do not allow it to boil. Let it simmer for about 5 minutes, then remove from the heat and set aside, remembering to stir occasionally.

Place the sugar and egg yolks in a mixing bowl and whisk together, using a hand or electric mixer, until you have a pale, thick and glossy paste.

Bring the milk mixture back up to a simmer, then gradually pour it into the egg mixture, whisking all the time, until it is well incorporated.

Return the mixture to the saucepan and cook for about 10 minutes on a low-to-medium heat, stirring constantly, to prevent it from curdling, until it has thickened enough to coat the back of the spoon.

Stir in the matcha powder and the lemon juice and cook on a low heat for a further 10 minutes to allow the flavours to infuse, giving the custard constant attention to avoid burning. Remove from heat.

Pour the custard into a bowl or large jug and leave it to cool at room temperature. Then place it in the refrigerator to chill for at least 1 hour.

Following the manufacturer's instructions, pour the chilled ice cream mixture into your ice cream maker and set it to churn. Once it has finished churning, decant the partially frozen ice cream into a freezer-friendly container and leave it in the freezer to set solid.

If you do not have an ice cream maker, follow the instructions on page 25.

Remove the ice cream from the freezer about 15 minutes before serving so that it can soften slightly.

# olive oil ice cream

**Lying happily somewhere between sweet and savoury, good-quality extra-virgin olive oil works on many levels and makes an ice cream which has great depth of flavour. Serve this intriguing concoction at the beginning of a meal as an amuse-bouche or between courses as a palate cleanser or, smothered in runny honey, as an after-dinner treat.**

250ml whole milk
250ml double cream
2 teaspoons fresh lemon juice
5 egg yolks
100g caster sugar
125ml extra-virgin olive oil

Pour the milk, cream and lemon juice into a saucepan and place over a low-to-medium heat. Bring to a simmer, stirring frequently to ensure that the mixture doesn't burn; do not allow it to boil. Let it simmer for about 5 minutes then remove from the heat and set aside, remembering to stir occasionally.

Place the egg yolks and sugar in a mixing bowl and whisk together, using a hand or electric mixer, until you have a pale, thick and glossy paste.

Bring the milk mixture back up to a simmer, then gradually pour it into the egg mixture, whisking all the time, until it is well incorporated.

Return the mixture to the saucepan and cook for about 10 minutes on a low-to-medium heat, stirring constantly, to prevent it from curdling, until it has thickened enough to coat the back of the spoon. Remove from heat and leave to cool.

Add the olive oil and re-whisk to incorporate fully.

Once cool, pour the mixture into a bowl or large jug, cover with cling film and place it in the refrigerator to chill for at least 1 hour.

Remove the chilled ice cream from the refrigerator and whisk again to ensure that the oil has not separated from the base mix.

Following the manufacturer's instructions, pour the mixture into your ice cream maker and set it to churn. Once it has finished churning, decant the partially frozen ice cream into a freezer-friendly container and leave it in the freezer to set solid.

If you do not have an ice cream maker, follow the instructions on page 25.

Remove the ice cream from the freezer about 15 minutes before serving so that it can soften slightly.

# *rhubarb crumble ice cream*

Here we have the ultimate contrast between sweet and sour: the sweet custard ice cream base offsetting the sharp tang of fresh rhubarb. The swirl of crumble adds a lovely textural contrast.

400g trimmed rhubarb
50ml cold water
150g vanilla sugar (page 39) or caster sugar
250ml whole milk
250ml double cream
5 free-range egg yolks

### For the crumble mix
150g plain flour
150g unsalted butter
100g caster sugar

First make the crumble mix. Preheat the oven to 120°C/Gas Mark $1/2$. Blend the flour and butter together in a food processor for a few minutes until they are thoroughly mixed, resembling breadcrumbs. Add the sugar and continue mixing for a few more minutes. The mixture should now resemble little pebble-like droplets.

Spread the mixture evenly over a baking tray and bake until golden brown. Set aside to cool for use later.

For the ice cream first roughly chop the rhubarb and submerge it in the water in a saucepan along with 50g of the sugar. Place over a medium heat, and cook for about 15–20 minutes, stirring occasionally, until it has broken down and reduced to a gloopy syrup. Remove from the heat and set aside to cool.

Pour the milk and cream into a saucepan and place over a low-to-medium heat. Bring to a simmer, stirring frequently to ensure that the mixture doesn't burn; do not allow it to boil. Let it simmer for about 5 minutes, then remove from the heat and set aside, remembering to stir occasionally.

Place the egg yolks and sugar in a mixing bowl and whisk together, using a hand or electric mixer, until you have a pale, thick and glossy paste.

Bring the milk mixture back up to a simmer, then gradually pour it into the egg mixture, whisking all the time, until it is well incorporated.

Return the mixture to the saucepan and cook for about 10 minutes on a low-to-medium heat, stirring constantly, to prevent it from curdling, until it has thickened enough to coat the back of the spoon. Remove from heat.

Whisk in half of the crumble and all of the rhubarb syrup. Place the pan back on a low heat and cook gently for another 5 minutes. Remove from heat.

Pour the mixture into a bowl or large jug and leave it to cool at room temperature. Then cover it with cling film and place it in the refrigerator for at least 1 hour to chill and let the flavours mature.

Following the manufacturer's instructions, pour the chilled mixture into your ice cream maker and set it to churn. Once it has finished churning, stir in the remaining crumble mix. Decant the partially frozen ice cream into a freezer-friendly container and leave it in the freezer to set solid.

If you do not have an ice cream maker, follow the instructions on page 25.

Remove the ice cream from the freezer about 15 minutes before serving so that it can soften slightly.

# *liquorice root and sherbert-coated ice cream*

Do you remember that childhood favourite, the Sherbet Fountain? As a child, they were my preferred sweet, and whenever Mum went to the post office she'd get one each for me and my brother. Tearing open the top of the paper wrapper would release a cloud of sherbet into your face and reveal a long stick of liquorice which you could then dip into the sherbet. This ice cream is my re-creation of that simple but amazing treat. Rolled and coated in sherbet, this liquorice ice cream also offers a caramel/toffee flavour thanks to the use of brown sugar.

200ml whole milk
300ml double cream
1 tablespoon liquorice root powder
5 free-range egg yolks
125g light brown sugar
3 tablespoons lemon sherbet powder

Pour the milk and cream into a saucepan, bring to a gentle simmer over a low-to-medium heat, then add the liquorice root powder. Cover the pan, turn the heat to the lowest possible setting, and leave for about 3 hours to allow flavour maturation.

Meanwhile, in a mixing bowl, whisk the egg yolks and sugar together, using a hand or electric mixer, until you have a pale, thick and glossy paste.

Bring the milk mixture back up to a simmer, then gradually pour it into the egg mixture, whisking all the time, until it is well incorporated.

Return the mixture to the saucepan and cook for about 10 minutes on a low-to-medium heat, stirring constantly, to prevent it from curdling, until it has thickened enough to coat the back of the spoon. Remove from heat and set aside to cool.

Now use an electric whisk to aerate the ice cream mixture for about 3–5 minutes.

Pour the mixture into a bowl or large jug and leave it to cool at room temperature. Then cover it with cling film and place it in the refrigerator to chill for at least 1 hour.

Following the manufacturer's instructions, pour the chilled ice cream mixture into your ice cream maker and set it to churn. Once it has finished churning, decant the partially frozen ice cream into a freezer-friendly container and leave it in the freezer to set solid.

If you do not have an ice cream maker, follow the instructions on page 25.

Remove the ice cream from the freezer about 15 minutes before serving so that it can soften slightly. When ready to serve, scoop the ice cream into generous-sized balls, and roll in the sherbet.

# *beetroot sorbet*

**In this refreshingly different, sophisticated sorbet, beetroot provides a sweet, earthy flavour. Thanks to its high water content the sorbet serves admirably as a palate cleanser between courses, and I often use it this way at dinner parties – its versatility making it the perfect partner for game or smoked meats.**

100g caster sugar
75ml water
125ml purchased beetroot juice
1 teaspoon lemon juice
1 tablespoon liquid glucose
1 sheet gelatine (20–25g)

Pour the sugar and water into a medium-sized saucepan, place over a medium heat and bring to a simmer. Continue to simmer, stirring, until the sugar has dissolved and the liquid becomes syrupy. Remove the pan from the heat and set aside to cool.

Once cool, pour the beetroot juice, lemon juice and liquid glucose into the syrup and mix together using a hand or electric whisk.

Soak the gelatine sheet in a shallow bowl or cup of cold water for 5 minutes, then squeeze out the excess water and add to the beetroot mix.

Return the mixture to a medium heat for 5 minutes to ensure that the gelatine has completely dissolved, then remove the saucepan from the heat.

Pour the mixture into a bowl or large jug and leave it to cool at room temperature. Then cover it with cling film and place it in the refrigerator to chill for at least 1 hour.

Pour the chilled mixture into your ice cream maker and set it to churn. Once it has finished churning, decant the partially frozen sorbet into a freezer-friendly container and leave it in the freezer to set solid.

If you do not have an ice cream maker, follow the instructions on page 25.

Remove the sorbet from the freezer about 15 minutes before serving so that it can soften slightly.

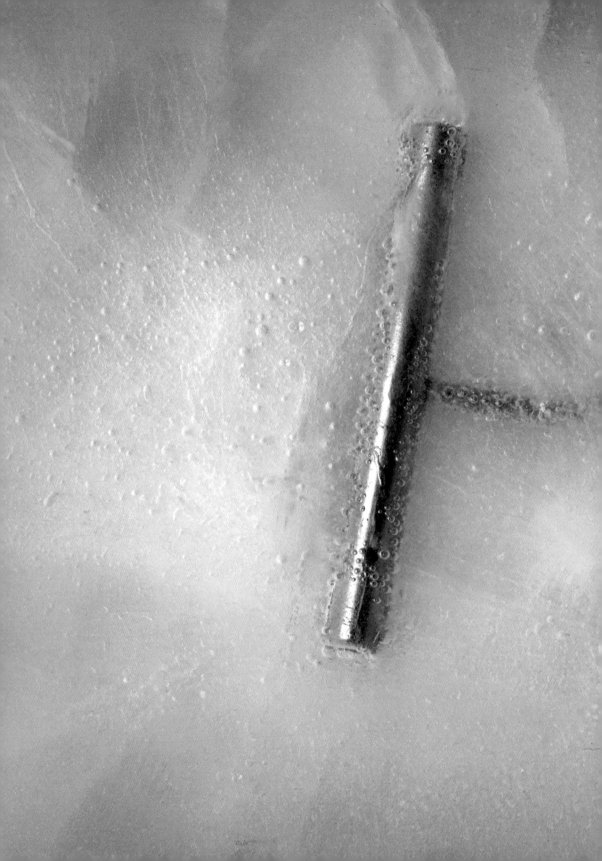

alcoholic
infusions

alcoh

Using alcohol in ice cream and sorbet gives greater depth of flavour and sophistication. It's important to get the quantity of alcohol correct: using too much of it will prevent your ice cream or sorbet from freezing properly, as I've found many times when developing a recipe. Conversely, using too little will produce an unbalanced recipe and an ice cream or sorbet that freezes too hard. Recipes in this chapter include classics such as Rum & Raisin and Guinness Ice Cream, as well as ice cream based on that Italian classic dessert Tiramisu and a Lemonade and Vodka Sorbet, which is perfect as a refreshing after-dinner treat.

To make a dark, flavoursome and delicious rum syrup, perfect for pouring over ice cream, especially Bourbon Vanilla (page 48), heat 100g of light brown sugar, 100ml water, 1 teaspoon of vanilla extract and 2 tablespoons of dark rum together in a saucepan over a medium heat.

Stir almost continuously until the sugar has fully dissolved into the liquid. This process should take no longer than 5 minutes, during which time the liquid will thicken to become a gloopy syrup. Remove the pan and set aside to cool and serve generously poured over the top of your ice cream.

# vanilla, rum and raisin ice cream

The subtle flavours of brown sugar, vanilla and molasses found within rum, make it an ideal ingredient for ice cream. A true classic – and one of my favourites – rum and raisin ice cream is bursting with flavour, given a textural 'kick' by the juicy raisins.

350ml double cream
200ml whole milk
60ml dark rum
1 vanilla pod
75g muscovado sugar
4 large free-range egg yolks
1 teaspoon fresh lemon juice
1 tablespoon Madagascan vanilla extract
100g large raisins

Pour the cream, milk and rum into a medium-sized saucepan. Using a sharp knife, split the vanilla pod lengthways and scrape out the seeds using the blunt edge of the knife. Add the pod and seeds to the saucepan and place over a low heat. Gently bring to a simmer, stirring frequently to ensure that the mixture doesn't burn; do not allow it to boil. Tip in half the sugar and continue to simmer until the sugar has fully dissolved. Let it simmer for about 5 minutes, then remove from the heat and set aside to allow the flavours to mature, remembering to stir occasionally.

Place the egg yolks and the remaining sugar in a mixing bowl and whisk together, using a hand or electric whisk, until you have a pale, thick and glossy paste.

Bring the milk mixture back up to a simmer, then gradually pour it into the egg mixture, whisking all the time, until it is well incorporated.

Return the mixture to the saucepan, add the lemon juice and the vanilla extract, and cook for about 10 minutes on a low-to-medium heat, stirring constantly, to prevent it from curdling, until it has thickened enough to coat the back of the spoon. Remove from heat and scoop out the vanilla pod.

Decant the mixture into a bowl or large jug and leave it to cool. Then cover with cling film and place in the refrigerator to chill for 24 hours, to allow a full-bodied flavour maturation to take place.

Remove from the fridge and whisk for up to 5 minutes using a hand whisk; this process will ensure that a small amount of air is incorporated into the ice cream base.

Pour the mixture into your ice cream maker and churn, following the manufacturer's instructions. Halfway through the process, stop the machine and throw in the raisins; then restart the machine and leave to finish churning. When this is complete, place the ice cream in a freezer-friendly container and put into the freezer to set solid.

Serve in generous-size scoops, preferably with a toffee sauce or maple syrup and a cold glass of dark rum on the rocks.

# gin and tonic sorbet

Gin has been a popular tipple for quite some time. Originally produced in Holland, it began to be distilled in England in the late seventeenth century. Like other spirits, beer and wine, gin (then very cheap) was widely consumed in preference to the generally unsafe water. Much later, gin played a supporting role in fighting malaria among British settlers in India. It was discovered that quinine, an ingredient of tonic water, could help to cure the disease. Adding a little gin to the tonic water made it more palatable, and so the gin and tonic was born. History aside, this summer drink makes for a refreshing and interesting sorbet. Serve it with a slice of lemon or lime.

200g caster sugar
125ml lemonade
300ml water
250ml tonic water
40–60ml gin (to taste)
2 tablespoons lemon juice

Put the sugar, lemonade and water into a saucepan, bring close to boiling point, then let simmer for 1 minute, or until the mixture thickens to a syrup. Set aside to cool, then add the tonic water and place in the fridge to chill for 30 minutes (note that the lemonade and tonic water will go slightly flat, but this will not affect the flavour).

Once the mixture has chilled, add the gin and the lemon juice to taste.

Following the manufacturer's instructions, pour the chilled sorbet mixture into your ice cream maker and set it to churn. Once it has finished churning, decant the partially frozen sorbet into a freezer-friendly container and leave it in the freezer to set solid.

If you do not have an ice cream maker, follow the instructions on page 25.

Remove the ice cream from the freezer about 15 minutes before serving so that it can soften slightly.

# *cointreau and orange sorbet*

**A sophisticated take on orange sorbet is achieved by adding the French orange-flavoured liqueur Cointreau. The result is a powerful yet refreshing sorbet that would feel at home at just about any dinner party.**

200g caster sugar
200ml water
1 teaspoon  lemon juice
400ml orange juice
3 tablespoons Cointreau

Pour the sugar and water into a saucepan and place over a medium heat. Bring close to boiling point, stirring occasionally; continue to let simmer – making sure the mixture does not boil – until all of the sugar has been dissolved and the liquid has a syrupy consistency.

Now remove the pan from the heat and gently stir in the lemon juice, orange juice and Cointreau. Return the pan to the heat and let simmer for a further 5 minutes to allow the flavours to infuse.

Remove the pan from the heat. Pour the mixture into a bowl or large jug and leave it to cool at room temperature. Then place it in the refrigerator to chill for at least 1 hour.

Following the manufacturer's instructions, pour the chilled sorbet mixture into your ice cream maker and set it to churn. Once it has finished churning, decant the partially frozen sorbet into a freezer-friendly container and leave it in the freezer to set solid.

If you do not have an ice cream maker, follow the instructions on page 25.

Remove the sorbet from the freezer about 15 minutes before serving so that it can soften slightly.

# *mulled cider sorbet*

**This recipe makes a really simple and quite special sorbet that's perfect for winter, being full of warming spices. Here cider provides the base, but this could be replaced with red wine, using the same measurements, or with port. For a non-alcoholic sorbet, substitute pressed apple juice.**

150g caster sugar
100ml water
juice and zest of 1 orange
juice and zest of 1 lemon
250ml sweet cider
1 teaspoon mixed spice
1 teaspoon cinnamon
1 free-range egg white

Pour the sugar and water into a saucepan and gently heat until close to boiling point, stirring gently. Then leave to simmer for 10 minutes, by which point the syrup should have thickened; simmer for a bit longer if necessary. Remove the pan from the heat and set aside to cool.

Pour the citrus juice and zest into a saucepan along with the cider and spices. Bring to a simmer and continue simmering gently for 5 minutes, then set aside to cool and allow the flavours to mature.

Combine the two liquids in a mixing bowl and place them in the fridge to chill for 1 hour. Then add the egg white and mix thoroughly with an electric or hand whisk.

Following the manufacturer's instructions, pour the chilled sorbet mixture into your ice cream maker and set it to churn. Once it has finished churning, decant the partially frozen sorbet into a freezer-friendly container and leave it in the freezer to set solid.

If you do not have an ice cream maker, follow the instructions on page 25.

Remove the sorbet from the freezer about 15 minutes before serving so that it can soften slightly.

# *guinness ice cream*

**Perhaps not surprisingly, the smooth and creamy Irish 'black gold', Guinness, makes a perfect ice cream. The ideal dessert choice for St Patrick's Day, Guinness ice cream can be enjoyed all year round. Try it as a complement to virtually any red meat dish.**

3 large free-range egg yolks
50g caster sugar
250ml whole milk
250ml double cream
200ml Guinness or similar milk stout

Whisk the egg yolks and sugar in a mixing bowl, using an electric whisk, for about 2 minutes, or until they form a pale, smooth paste.

Transfer the mixture to a saucepan and gently heat over a low heat for 2–3 minutes, stirring the mixture almost constantly to avoid burning it. Remove from the heat.

In a separate saucepan gently begin to heat the milk and cream to a simmer, stirring almost constantly to prevent it from burning; do not let it come to the boil. Slowly pour in the Guinness and stir vigorously for 5 minutes to make sure the ingredients are adequately combined.

Gradually pour the milk and Guinness mixture into the egg mixture, whisking all the time to avoid curdling. Return the pan to the heat and continue to stir until the mixture is fully combined and has thickened enough to coat the back of a spoon.

Pour the mixture into a bowl or large jug and leave it to cool at room temperature. Then place it in the refrigerator to chill for at least 1 hour.

Following the manufacturer's instructions, pour the chilled ice cream mixture into your ice cream maker and set it to churn. Once it has finished churning, decant the partially frozen ice cream into a freezer-friendly container and leave it in the freezer to set solid.

If you do not have an ice cream maker, follow the instructions on page 25.

Remove the ice cream from the freezer about 15 minutes before serving so that it can soften slightly.

# sloe gin and damson ice cream

I should make a confession: this flavour is perhaps my favourite. Well loved in our household, it also impresses our guests. Damsons come into season around the end of summer and can still be found growing freely in hedgerows until the beginning of winter. Similar to plums, with a deep, rich purple hue, they combine beautifully with sloe gin, producing a tart, deep flavour. If you can't find damsons, you can substitute the same quantity of plums.

5 free-range egg yolks
150g caster sugar plus a little extra
100g damsons, washed and stones removed
3 tablespoons sloe gin
250ml whole milk
350ml double cream

In a mixing bowl beat together the egg yolks and 150g sugar using an electric whisk. Continue whisking until they form a glossy, pale and smooth paste. Set this aside for later.

Now purée the fruit. Roughly chop the damsons and place in a saucepan, cover with a few teaspoons of sugar, the sloe gin and a few tablespoons of cold water. Cover and place over a medium heat for 5 minutes, then remove the lid and stir; the fruit should have begun to break down by this point. Return to the heat for another 5 minutes, uncovered; the mixture should have thickened to form a syrup. Set aside to cool.

Pour the cooled cooked damsons into a blender or food processor, and blend until free of lumps. Now pour through a fine sieve into a clean saucepan; set aside to allow flavours to infuse.

Pour the milk and cream into another saucepan and place over a low-to-medium heat. Bring it to a simmer, stirring frequently and watching carefully to avoid boiling or burning the mixture.

Gradually pour the hot milk mixture into the egg mixture, whisking all the time, until it is well incorporated.

Return the mixture to the saucepan and cook for 5–10 minutes on a low–medium heat, stirring constantly to prevent it from curdling until it has thickened enough to coat the back of the spoon.

Now stir in the damson purée (scrape the bottom of the pan to ensure the mixtures have combined) and whisk with an electric whisk for about 5 minutes.

Pour the mixture into a bowl or large jug and leave it to cool at room temperature. Then cover it with cling film and place it in the refrigerator to chill for at least 1 hour.

Following the manufacturer's instructions, pour the chilled mixture into your ice cream maker and set it to churn. Once it has finished churning, decant the partially frozen ice cream into a freezer-friendly container and leave it in the freezer to set solid.

If you do not have an ice cream maker, follow the instructions on page 25.

Remove the ice cream from the freezer about 15 minutes before serving so that it can soften slightly.

# *lemonade and vodka sorbet*

A sweet, cleansing sorbet with a kick, this is a very simple recipe; but for good results, make sure to follow the alcohol measurement to the letter. For extra flavour, add the zest of an unwaxed lemon.

175g caster sugar
350ml cold water
1 teaspoon lemon juice
3 tablespoons vodka
50ml lemonade

Gently heat the sugar and water in a saucepan over a medium heat, stirring, until the sugar has completely dissolved, leaving a thick, glossy syrup. Bring to a simmer and leave simmering, without stirring, for 5 minutes.

Now add the lemon juice, vodka and lemonade and continue simmering for a further 5 minutes. Remove from the heat.

Pour the mixture into a bowl or large jug and leave it to cool at room temperature. Then place it in the refrigerator to chill for at least 1 hour.

Following the manufacturer's instructions, pour the chilled sorbet mixture into your ice cream maker and set it to churn. Once it has finished churning, decant the partially frozen sorbet into a freezer-friendly container and leave it in the freezer to set solid.

If you do not have an ice cream maker, follow the instructions on page 25.

Remove the sorbet from the freezer about 15 minutes before serving so that it can soften slightly.

Serve the sorbet in small scoops (made with a melon baller) in shot glasses.

# *tiramisu ice cream*

**This ice cream is a tribute to one of the most iconic Italian desserts of recent times. As in the original dish, layers of mascarpone, cream, sugar, coffee, chocolate and marsala (plus amaretto) all come together to create a powerful, deep and instantly recognisable taste experience – perfectly finished off with a light dusting of cocoa powder.**

150g caster sugar
5 tablespoons marsala
450g mascarpone
250ml double cream
5 tablespoons amaretto liqueur
2 teaspoons fresh lemon juice
5 tablespoons freshly ground coffee
50g dark chocolate, roughly chopped

In a mixing bowl beat together the sugar, marsala and mascarpone using an electric whisk; continue whisking until the ingredients are fully combined and the mixture is slightly aerated.

Pour the double cream, amaretto, lemon juice and ground coffee into a saucepan and place over a medium heat until all the ingredients are fully combined and the mixture is thick enough to coat the back of a spoon. Set aside to cool.

Temper the chocolate as instructed on page 111 and set it aside to cool. Once cool, fold it into the cream mixture.

Now fold the cream mixture into the slightly aerated mascarpone mixture and set in the fridge to chill for at least 1 hour.

Following the manufacturer's instructions, pour the chilled ice cream mixture into your ice cream maker and set it to churn. Once it has finished churning, decant the partially frozen ice cream into a freezer-friendly container and leave it in the freezer to set solid.

If you do not have an ice cream maker, follow the instructions on page 25.

Remove the ice cream from the freezer about 15 minutes before serving so that it can soften slightly.

Serve the ice cream in generous scoops with a light dusting of cocoa powder.

# *champagne and elderflower sorbet*

The flower of the elderberry shrub, in season from May through to July, is loved for its sweet fragrant flavour. This sorbet is a wonderfully clean and refreshing dessert.

25ml elderflower cordial
2 tablespoons lemon juice
250ml water
150g caster sugar
250ml Champagne or sparkling white wine

Gently heat the elderflower cordial, lemon juice, water and sugar in a saucepan over a medium heat, stirring, until the sugar has completely dissolved, leaving a thick, gloopy syrup. Bring to a simmer and leave simmering for 5 minutes.

Remove from the heat. Once cool, pour the Champagne into the syrup and stir well to combine.

Pour the mixture into a bowl or large jug and leave it to cool at room temperature. Then cover with cling film and place it in the refrigerator to chill for at least 1 hour.

Following the manufacturer's instructions, pour the chilled sorbet mixture into your ice cream maker and set it to churn. Once it has finished churning, decant the partially frozen sorbet into a freezer-friendly container and leave it in the freezer for 4 or 5 hours to set solid.

If you do not have an ice cream maker, follow the instructions on page 25.

Remove the sorbet from the freezer about 15 minutes before serving so that it can soften slightly.

# *apple cider lolly*

As a child, enjoying the privilege of growing up at the family ice cream parlour, I had a special fondness for cider lollies and in the summertime would often help myself to one of these treats from the cold stores. I was innocently unaware that their sweet, sharp taste was achieved largely by artificial flavourings and stabilisers. As a grown-up I now prefer my cider lollies to be made of natural ingredients – including plenty of booze.

### *makes 15 ice lollies or 20 ice cubes*

500ml dry cider
125g caster sugar
1 tablespoon lemon juice
1 tablespoon lime juice

Pour half of the cider into small saucepan and bring to a rapid boil, continue for 15 minutes to allow the liquid to reduce by 50 per cent. Now remove from the heat and set aside to cool.

Once cool, stir in the sugar, lemon juice and lime juice; return the pan to a medium heat and pour in the remaining cider. Bring to a simmer, stirring constantly to help the sugar dissolve and to stop the mixture from burning. Continue to heat for 5 minutes, then remove from the heat and set aside to cool.

Pour the cooled mixture into lolly moulds or ice cube trays. If using moulds allow a 1cm clearance at the top to allow for a small amount of expansion. Place the lollies/ice cubes in the freezer to set solid.

# orange and prosecco lolly

Here prosecco adds a little fizz and sophistication to an otherwise ordinary ice lolly. Alternatively the mixture could be frozen in ice cube trays and used to sweeten or add sparkle to a drink.

*makes 15 ice lollies or 20 ice cubes*

500ml prosecco or other sparkling white wine
2 tablespoons orange juice
125g caster sugar

Pour half of the prosecco into a small saucepan and bring to a rapid boil, continue for 15 minutes to allow the liquid to reduce by 50 per cent. Remove from the heat and set aside to cool.

Once cool, stir in the orange juice and sugar, return the pan to a medium heat and pour in the remaining prosecco. Bring to a simmer, stirring constantly to help the sugar dissolve and to prevent the mixture from burning. Continue to heat for 5 more minutes, then remove from the heat and set aside to cool.

Pour the cooled mixture into the lolly moulds or ice cube trays. (When pouring into moulds allow a 1cm clearance at the top to allow for a small amount of expansion.) Place in the freezer to set solid.

# absinthe ice lollies

Banned across much of Europe and America until recent years, absinthe was thought to be dangerously addictive and mind altering, which, coupled with its distinctive vivid green colour, led to its nickname, 'the green fairy'. Undoubtedly strong in alcoholic content, absinthe is a wonderful botanical blend of fennel, wormwood, green anise and sugar. Mixed with Midori and freshly squeezed lime juice, it makes an amazing ice lolly.

*makes 12–15 lollies*

150g caster sugar
500ml cold water
50ml absinthe
75ml Midori melon liqueur
2 tablespoons lime juice

Pour the sugar and cold water into a saucepan, place over a medium heat and bring to a simmer, whisking frequently with a hand whisk. Continue to simmer, whisking, for 10 minutes, until the sugar has fully dissolved and the liquid turns syrupy.

Remove the saucepan from the heat and set aside to cool for 10 minutes. Now stir in the absinthe, Midori and lime juice until all of the ingredients are fully combined. Decant the mixture to a mixing bowl, cover with cling film and place in the fridge to chill for 1 hour.

Remove the chilled mixture from the fridge, transfer to a jug and decant into lolly moulds, leaving 1cm space at the top of each mould for the liquid to expand slightly. Place in the freezer for 2 hours to partially set.

Remove the moulds from the freezer to insert the sticks, if necessary, then place the lollies back in the freezer for at least 12 hours to set solid. (The lollies take longer to set than most ice cream/sorbet due to their relatively high alcohol content.)

*accompaniments*

*accompa*

Although ice cream is delicious on its own, there's no denying that a bit of crunch will set it off. You can buy biscuits, meringues and even cones from a shop, but surely your lovely home-made ice cream deserves to be partnered by something just as special, also your own creation. In the following pages you'll find a selection of ideas to give your ice cream star treatment.

You will learn the art of making perfect meringue nests, crisp tuiles, brandy snaps and sugar-spun baskets. This chapter also provides an in-depth guide to making three wonderful types of cone. A special kind of waffle iron will allow you to make those cones (pictured in the following pages). With an ordinary waffle iron, though, you can make traditional waffles which can be topped with ice cream. To make a simple waffle, get a mixing bowl and beat together 250g sifted plain flour, 2 eggs, 10g baking powder, 20g caster sugar, 1 teaspoon vanilla extract, 450ml whole milk and 30ml olive oil. Mix the ingredients until they are well combined. Pre-heat your waffle iron, greasing it with oil, and pour $3/4$ of the batter onto the iron and cook for 4 or 5 minutes until it is golden brown. It will be delicious served with lashings of golden syrup, a few generous scoops of ice cream and slices of banana. These waffles can be stored for up to two weeks in a sealed container or frozen in a freezer-safe container for up to 2 months.

# *simple sugar cone*

The symbol of summer holidays at the seaside – an ice cream cornet, with a generous dollop of ice cream on top – c an easily be replicated at home, using this simple recipe.

### *makes 4 cones, about 18cm tall*

2 large, free-range egg whites
1 tablespoon vanilla extract
100g caster sugar
100g plain flour
pinch of salt
50g unsalted butter, melted

Preheat the oven to 180°C/Gas Mark 4.

Have ready 2 baking trays lined with baking parchment and a cone form. If you cannot get a ready-made form, you can make one, as follows: using a salad plate, or similar, as a template, draw a circle on a piece of flexible card and cut it out. Roll it into a cone shape, making the bottom hole as small as possible, and fasten with tape. Cover the outside with a piece of kitchen foil.

In a mixing bowl, using a hand or electric whisk, mix together the egg whites, vanilla, and caster sugar until fully combined. Stir in the flour, salt and melted butter; continue to stir until the mix becomes smooth.

Line 2 baking trays with baking parchment. Using a ladle, pour 2 ladlefuls of batter on to each tray, spacing them well apart. Using a butter knife or palette knife, evenly spread the batter into 4 circles, each about 18–20cm across.

Place one baking tray in the centre of the oven and cook the batter circles for about 15 minutes, or until golden brown. Remove from the oven and leave to cool slightly. Repeat with the other tray.

After about 5 minutes of cooling time, gently lay the cone form on one of the circles, with the point just in from the edge, and carefully wrap the circle around it. With the join underneath, press down on the cone to seal the edges; pinch the bottom to prevent a hole. Slide the cone off the form and set it aside to cool.

Set the cones aside to cool for use when needed. They will keep for up to 2 weeks in a sealed container.

# waffle cone

The waffle cone was popularised at the beginning of the 1900s after the traditional 'penny lick' was banned due to hygiene concerns. It is baked in a special waffle iron with a shallow grid (see page 34) and then hand-rolled around an conical shape. (Many waffle irons come with cone forms included; if yours does not, follow the instructions for home-made forms on page 263.) The addition of different sugars, flavourings and even food colouring, can provide interesting results and variations – liquorice waffle cones, made popular by the London ice cream parlour The Icecreamists is a fine example.

### makes 6–8 cones, about 20cm tall

4 egg whites
a squeeze of lemon juice
150g caster sugar
100g plain flour, sifted
a pinch of salt
50g unsalted butter, melted
sunflower oil, for greasing

In a mixing bowl, using a hand or electric whisk, mix together the egg whites, lemon juice and caster sugar until fully combined. Stir in the flour, salt and melted butter and continue to stir until the mixture becomes smooth.

Grease the waffle iron and heat it, following the manufacturer's instructions, then pour the batter on to it. Cook for the specified time until crisp and golden.

Remove the waffle from the iron and leave it on a flat surface to cool slightly for about 3 minutes. Then lay a cone form on the waffle with the point near the edge of the waffle and carefully roll the waffle around the form. (First placing the waffle on a cloth and using that to help roll will protect your hands if sensitive to the heat.) With the overlapped edge underneath, press down on the waffle, still in the form to seal the join. Pinch the bottom to seal the hole. Slide the cone off the form and set it aside to cool.

The cones will keep in a sealed container for up to 2 weeks.

# *wholemeal waffle cone*

A surprisingly moreish alternative to the traditional waffle cone, this recipe uses wholemeal self-raising flour, which produces a much denser batter, and brown sugar, which gives the waffle a delicious caramel flavour.

*makes 6–8 cones, about 20cm tall*

3 egg whites
1 teaspoon vanilla extract
150g light brown sugar
a pinch of salt
100g unsalted butter, melted
100g wholemeal self-raising flour, sifted
sunflower oil, for greasing

In a mixing bowl, using a hand or electric whisk, mix together the egg whites, vanilla, and light brown sugar until fully combined. Stir into the mix the salt, melted butter and sifted flour, continue to stir until the mix becomes smooth.

Grease the waffle iron and heat it, following the manufacturer's instructions, then pour the batter on to it. Cook for the specified time until crisp and golden brown.

Remove the waffle from the iron and leave it on a flat surface to cool slightly for about 3 minutes. Then lay a cone form on the waffle with the point near the edge of the waffle and carefully roll the waffle around the form. (First placing the waffle on a cloth and using that to help roll will protect your hands if sensitive to the heat.) With the overlapped edge underneath, press down on the waffle, still in the form to seal the join. Pinch the bottom to seal the hole. Slide the cone off the form and set it aside to cool.

If you do not have a waffle iron, follow the instructions for baking in the oven given for Simple Sugar Cone on page 263, where you will also find instructions for making a cardboard cone form.

The cones will keep for up to 2 weeks in a sealed container.

# *brandy snap basket*

**Traditionally moulded into a tubular shape and filled with whipped cream, often infused with brandy (hence the name), brandy snaps can also be formed into a dish or basket shape, making a pretty – and edible – little nest for ice cream.**

*makes 4 baskets*

sunflower oil, for greasing
2 tablespoons vanilla sugar (see page 39)
30g butter
1 tablespoon golden syrup
30g plain flour
a large pinch of nutmeg
a large pinch of ground ginger

Preheat the oven to 190°C/Gas Mark 5.

Line two baking trays with baking parchment. Grease the outsides of 4 individual pudding basins or large ramekins with sunflower oil and place them upside down on a flat surface.

Place the vanilla sugar, butter and golden syrup in a saucepan over a low heat, and cook, stirring occasionally to stop the butter from burning, for 5 minutes, or until all of the ingredients have melted and are fully combined.

Remove the pan from the heat and set aside to cool, stirring the mixture occasionally until cool.

Sift the flour into the cooled butter mixture, add the nutmeg and ginger, and stir until all of the ingredients are well combined.

Using a large dessertspoon, drop 2 rounded spoonfuls of the brandy snap mixture on to each baking sheet, spacing them well apart. Bake for 5–6 minutes until golden, then remove from the oven and leave to begin cooling.

While the snaps are still warm, use a flat butter knife or a palette knife to lift each one on to a greased basin; gently mould it around the basin to make a dish shape. Leave the snaps to cool for 5 minutes, then lift them off and set them aside for use presently; or stack in a sealed plastic container, where they will keep for up to 2 weeks.

# *meringue nests*

Perfect meringues are a glistening, brilliant white, with a stiff, crisp exterior and a soft, chewy interior. Achieving this degree of perfection is not easy, but if you follow my instructions carefully you should achieve good results. Meringues can be simply placed in mounds on the baking sheet and then broken up for use in various ice cream recipes, such as Eton Mess Ice Cream (page 142), or, as shown here, formed into little nests in which to serve your ice cream.

### *makes 5 or 6 meringue nests, about 12–13cm in diameter*

4 free-range egg whites, at room temperature
1 teaspoon vanilla extract
100g vanilla sugar (see page 39)

First line a baking sheet with baking parchment. Preheat the oven to 140°C/Gas Mark 1.

Place the egg whites in a mixing bowl (first making sure it is absolutely clean – any grease will inhibit volume). Using an electric whisk on a low speed, whisk for about 2–5 minutes, until the egg whites are foamy; then add the vanilla extract, increase the speed to medium and continue whisking for another minute.

Increase the speed to maximum and continue whisking until the egg whites become stiff, glossy peaks, then whisk in the sugar a little at a time until the texture becomes even more stiff and glossy.

Leave the mixture to rest for a moment, then scoop out 5 or 6 heaped dessertspoons of the stiff egg whites and place them on the lined baking sheet. Hollow out the centres using the back of the dessertspoon.

Place the baking tray in the centre of the oven and bake for 25 minutes. Then turn off the oven and leave the meringues to dry out in the warmth of the oven until it is has cooled completely; this may take up to 2 hours.

Remove the meringues from the oven and place in a sealed plastic container; they will keep fresh here for up to 2 weeks.

# spun-sugar basket

These lacy, intricate spun-sugar baskets aren't half as difficult to make as they look. Sitting on a plate and filled with a few small scoops of ice cream or sorbet, they provide instant visual impact and add a delightfully crunchy texture as you eat them.

**makes 5 good-sized baskets**

200g golden syrup
250g granulated sugar
2 teaspoons cold water

In a saucepan, gently heat the golden syrup, the sugar and the water; bring to a simmer, then leave simmering for 10 minutes, or until the temperature of the sugar syrup reaches 150°C (300°F).

Place an upturned breakfast cereal bowl, covered with cling film, on a chopping board. Using a large fork, quickly and repeatedly dip this into the syrup and wave it over the bowl.

Quickly begin building up fine layers of sugar over the bowl, so that the bowl is eventually encased in spun-sugar syrup. Set the bowl aside in a cool, dry area of the kitchen to allow the syrup to solidify. Then gently remove the basket from the bowl. Use the basket as a container for ice cream, gelato or sorbet.

The baskets will keep in a sealed container for up to 6 weeks.

# *tuiles*

So called for their resemblance to the curved terracotta roof tiles traditionally used on French houses, tuiles are crisp, sweet wafers that serve as a superb accompaniment to ice cream and sorbet. Flavoured with vanilla extract and ground almonds, these tuiles are very simple and quick to make at home.

### *makes 12 tuiles*

100g caster sugar
75g plain flour
2 egg whites
2 teaspoons vanilla extract
2 tablespoons ground almonds

Preheat the oven to 200°C/Gas Mark 6. Grease a baking tray with butter or line it with baking parchment.

Place all the ingredients in a mixing bowl and mix them together with an electric whisk until they are fully combined. The mixture should bind together into a thick, lumpy mass.

Using a spatula or spoon, place 12 small portions on the baking tray and spread them into rounds.

Bake the tuiles on a middle shelf for 8 minutes, or until golden brown around the edges.

Remove the tray from the oven and, using a spatula, pick up each tuile and drape it over the handle of the spatula to form the tuile's uneven basket shape. Leave the tuiles to cool on a flat surface; they will cool very quickly.

The tuiles can be stored in a sealed container for up to 2 weeks.

*and
finally...*

# 21st-century whippy

I couldn't finish this book without giving you my take on the ice cream which, for most of us, formed our first taste of the enchanted riches of this wonderful frozen dessert...

As a child, who didn't love a Mr Whippy ice cream? The two key elements of a Mr Whippy – the visual impact of its towering, twirling shape and its soft, light, airy texture – are retained in this recipe here. I've developed a very light, elastic base mix, which I whisk at top speed, freeze and finally blend in a food processor. The use of a piping bag produces the classic 'Whippy' shape. In 2012, I was asked to work with Heston Blumenthal and Walls Ice Cream as part of a Channel 4 series to help create the world's largest Mr Whippy, injecting flavour and quality into a novelty that had otherwise lacked such things. I can assure you that this Mr Whippy will be devoured a whole lot quicker than the one we made with Heston took!

500ml double cream
250ml whole milk
2 teaspoons vanilla extract
1 leaf pectin or gelatine (20–25g)
1 teaspoon skimmed milk powder
120g vanilla sugar (see page 39) or caster
   sugar

*note: you will need ice cube trays containing at least 30 spaces*

In a medium saucepan, heat the double cream milk and vanilla over a low heat and bring to a gentle simmer, stirring constantly and making sure the mixture does not boil. When it reaches the simmering point, add the pectin/gelatine leaf and stir until fully dissolved.

Add the milk powder and sugar and stir until fully dissolved. At this stage you should begin to notice the mixture thickening up. If it is not thick enough to coat the back of a spoon, add a further teaspoon of sugar and heat for a few more minutes.

Once the mixture has thickened adequately, pour it into a mixing bowl and set it aside to cool. Once cool, place it in the refrigerator to chill for 1 hour. Then whisk for 5 minutes using an electric whisk at full speed. Decant the mixture into ice cube trays and place in the freezer to set solid.

Once solid, place the cubes of ice cream in a blender or food processor and blend at full speed until you have a partially frozen paste. Pour this into a piping bag and pipe onto cones. Voilà! Perfect homemade 'Whippy' ice cream without any of the bad stuff.

# *index*

# *acknowledgements*

I left the world of city banking behind five years ago. Little did I know then that the years which followed would be one long, non-stop rollercoaster – full of the highest highs and the lowest lows. Throughout that time some fantastic people have been there with love and support and to provide opportunities to help ensure the success of Winstone's Ice Cream and to further me in all of my other endeavours too. Set against the backdrop of the day-to-day craziness which comes with being involved with such a busy family-run ice-cream firm, there has been the creation of this book – and it has been a fantastic journey from start to finish.

When I first met the teams at Absolute Press and Bloomsbury, I explained how I wanted to create a unique book, one which was very different to anything else out there. I had no idea that I would be encouraged to aim so much higher. This, then, is the book I always wanted to write yet which came to surpass even my wild dreams!

Without wanting this to sound too much like an Oscar speech, this book would simply not have been possible without the help of the following people…

Firstly, I must thank the beautiful Veena, who helps my feet stay firmly on the ground and assists my parents, Jane and Colin and Steve, in supporting me, inspiring me and spurring me on. Most importantly, she also ensures my ego is kept in check at all times!

My brother, Tom, who keeps hold of the reigns so capably at the family firm, when I've been busy baking, ice-cream making, writing, researching and with all other manner of book- and media-based activity.

For the amazing support and forward thinking of publisher, Jon Croft, and art director, Matt Inwood, at the small but mighty Absolute Press office in Bath, and thanks too to Absolute's commissioning editor, Meg Avent, and project editor, Alice Gibbs. The whole team at Bloomsbury Publishing have placed their faith in me, and given me their time and resources and shown great patience. They've given me an opportunity which I have grasped with both hands and will go on embracing.

Sue Lister at ListerComms has been a fantastic help in providing me with a brilliant Magimix Gelato home ice-cream making machine, without which this book would not have been possible – I highly recommended it!

The whole team at Divine Chocolate – especially Charlotte Borger – have been very supportive and have provided me with so much chocolate knowledge which has been invaluable throughout a number of my recipes.

My photographer, Mike Cooper, and food stylist, Genevieve Taylor, have so carefully and lovingly brought this book to life through their hard work, creativity and a sheer dedication to creating the most stunning looking ice cream book there is.

There is a very special thank you to my

trusty, official supporting snapper Tammy Lynn Kwan, based in Stroud, Gloucestershire.

And also a thank you to photographer Jessica Beveridge who joined me for a summery day of photography as this book was just beginning.

For pearls of wisdom and advice, Emily Knight at Bristol Bites; Dan Ingram, formerly of the Red Lion in Cricklade; and the Cotswold Chef, Rob Rees, have all provided me with focus, direction and advice whenever needed and have inspired many of my recipes.

In helping to test these recipes, I must tip my hat to Emma Bradshaw, Jo Lawson, Fiona Ridley, Dolores Bowskill, Chris Fowler, Urvashi Roe, Helen Best-Shaw, Alice Paling, Marcus Green, Catherine Green, Mark Glynne Jones, Jules Telford, Angie Petkovic, the team at Wholefoods (including Ren Rees, Angie, Peter and Mary), and many others who have helped champion me in the last twelve months or so.

I also wanted to mention and give thanks to some of my favourite authors, including Niki Segnit whose *Flavour Theasuarus* has taught me a whole new mantra of cooking; Philip Dundas, author of the remarkable *Cooking without Recipes* – a really great inspiration and entirely new concept in cookery; and finally Vanessa Kimbell, the author of *Prepped!*, whose own book journey inspired me to take the first tentative steps on the road to my own first book. Vanessa is not only a superbly warm, knowledgeable and talented cook, but she is also a reliable and trustworthy friend to who I wish every success in her own writing career.